PARANORMAL SUNDERLAND

STEVE WATSON

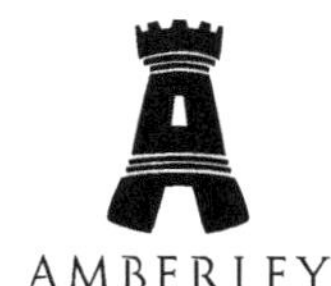

AMBERLEY

First published 2022

Amberley Publishing
The Hill, Stroud
Gloucestershire, GL5 4EP

www.amberley-books.com

British Library Cataloguing in Publication Data.
A catalogue record for this book is available from the British Library.

ISBN 978 1 3981 1051 9 (print)
ISBN 978 1 3981 1052 6 (ebook)

Typesetting by SJmagic DESIGN SERVICES, India.
Printed in Great Britain.

Appointed GPSR EU Representative: Easy Access System Europe Oü,
16879218
Address: Mustamäe tee 50, 10621, Tallinn, Estonia
Contact Details: gpsr.requests@easproject.com, +358 40 500 3575

Contents

Introduction

Writing a paranormal book about Sunderland really got me excited. I've spent many Saturdays on Wearside watching 'the lads' at both Roker Park and now at the Stadium of Light. During my childhood my dad would have to take me through to Sunderland every few weeks to watch Sunderland play. Being from Newcastle and my family being Toon supporters it must have broken his heart when I decided I wasn't going to follow the Magpies but wanted to wear red and white stripes. However, he would still smile and cheer with his youngest son as we would sit in the Old Clock Stand in the freezing cold with rain coming off the North Sea.

As I hit my teens, I would travel through to Sunderland on a Saturday by myself on the rickety old X19 bus from Cramlington – a two-hour bus ride each way. I'd arrive in Sunderland at lunchtime and wander around the city until making my way to the ground for kick-off. I had a keen interest in history back then and would look around the old buildings and have a wander down to the riverside. On some days, the occasional days when the temperature was above freezing, I'd have a walk down to the mouth of the Wear and watch as the ships bobbed by on the horizon.

And now, over forty years from my first attendance, you will still find me on most Saturday afternoons at the stadium with my children, still cheering on 'the lads' as I'm a real glutton for punishment.

The knowledge I gained about the area in those days really helped me over the past decade as I launched GHOSTnortheast, our local paranormal group. I already had thoughts about what locations I would want to investigate since I had heard many ghost stories during my time in Sunderland. Some locations opened their doors, and some said it wasn't for them. Unfortunately, some just don't exist anymore as they have made way for more modern buildings and developments. However, the stories of ghosts, ghouls and other scary beings are vast due to the history of the city.

Sunderland dates back to the Bronze Age. We know this as settlements have been discovered by archaeological digs all over the banks of the Wear. But it wasn't until the seventh century that Sunderland really made a name for itself and became noticeable in the history books.

The first district of the city as we know it today was built on the northern banks of the river when Benedict Biscop erected his monastery, and the area was aptly named Monkwearmouth. The monastery was the home of the Venerable Bede, who later built and twinned Monkwearmouth with his Jarrow monastery that was 10 miles north on the banks of the Tyne, becoming the Monkwearmouth-Jarrow Abbey.

With the growing popularity of the monasteries, Benedict Biscop was granted extra land by the king. He was given the land on the opposite side of the river, which would become known as 'the land that is separated'. A word meaning separated is sundered, hence the name 'Sunder-Land'.

The third district was built just before the turn of the first millennium. It was built to the west of Sunderland and named Bishopwearmouth.

Over the centuries, after the monasteries had gone, Sunderland was recognised for its fishing trade. The North Sea was home to some of the finest cod and herring, while further up the Wear was home to salmon. The river would continue to be the source of income to the growing town as shipbuilding began on its banks. The industry would last for nearly 600 years, until the late twentieth century. The ships would provide transport for the growing salt and coal industries that the North would rely on over the next 500 years.

But in the late twentieth century, the region would see a major decline in its industry. The coal mines were closed and the shipbuilding stopped, which has meant that the city has had to regenerate itself with new businesses and enterprises, with Nissan probably being the most notable.

As you can see, the history is as fascinating as the ghost stories. I recount the following tales as they have been told to me. Whether they are true, folklore or even an overly active imagination after a few pints before kick-off, I will let you decide.

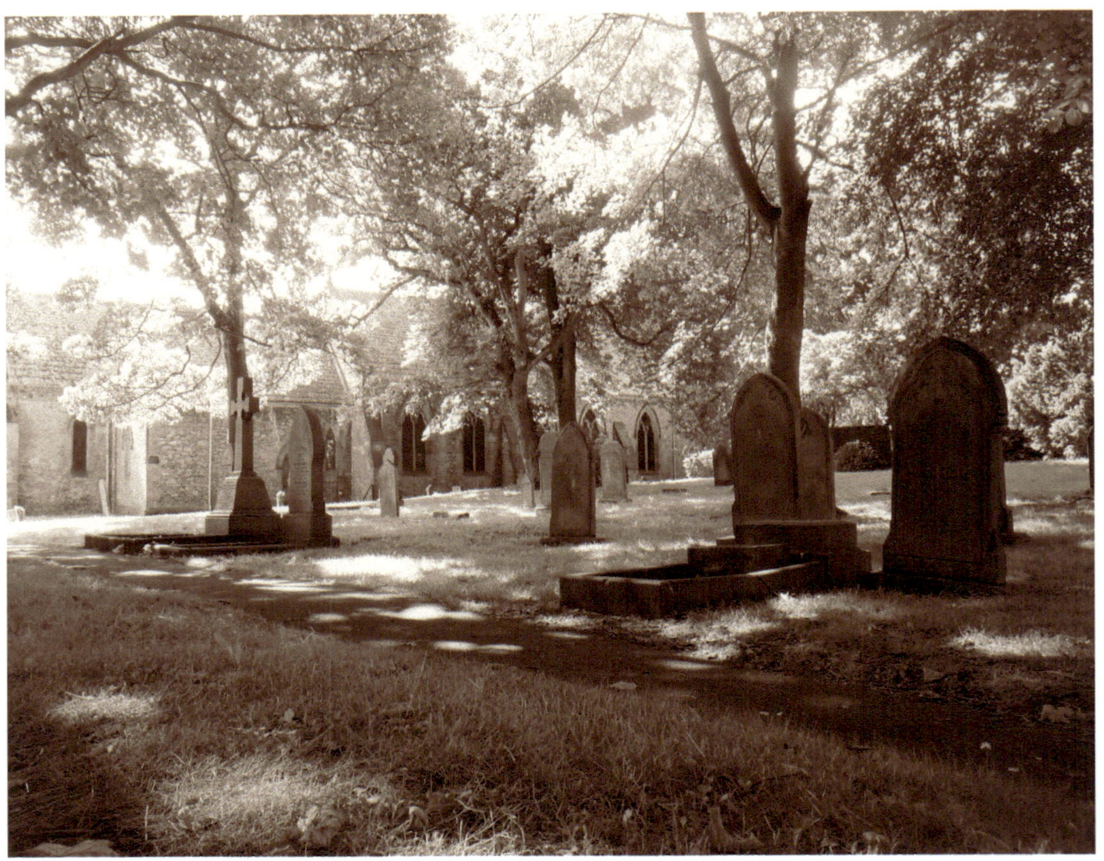

Old graveyards are dotted around Wearside.

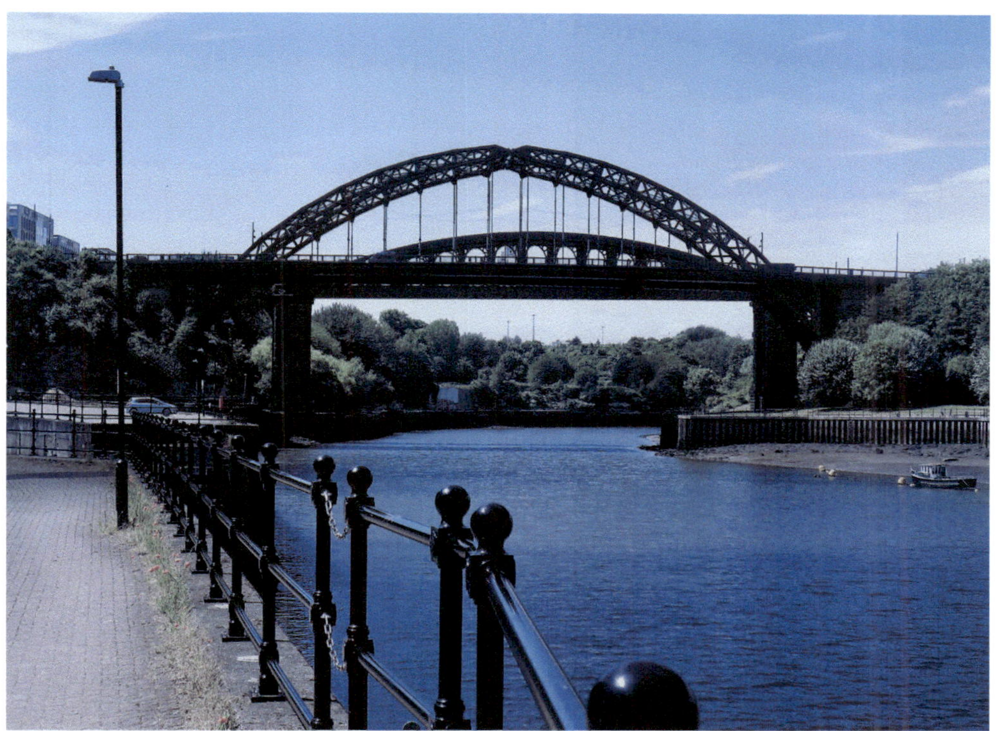

The famous Wearmouth Bridge.

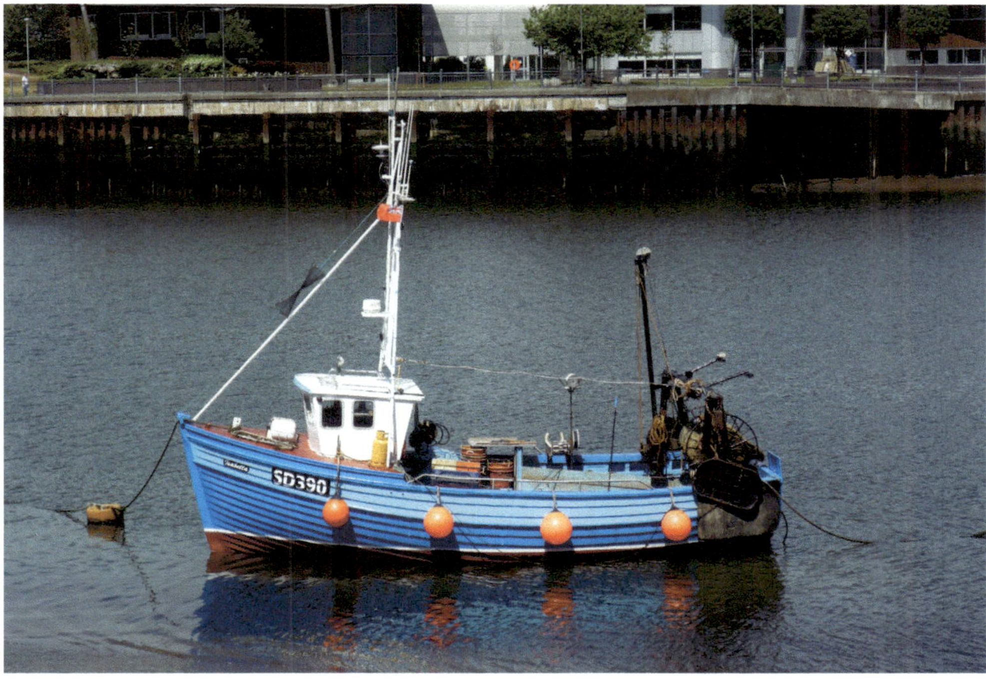

Boats have always been important to the people of Sunderland.

          Paranormal Sunderland

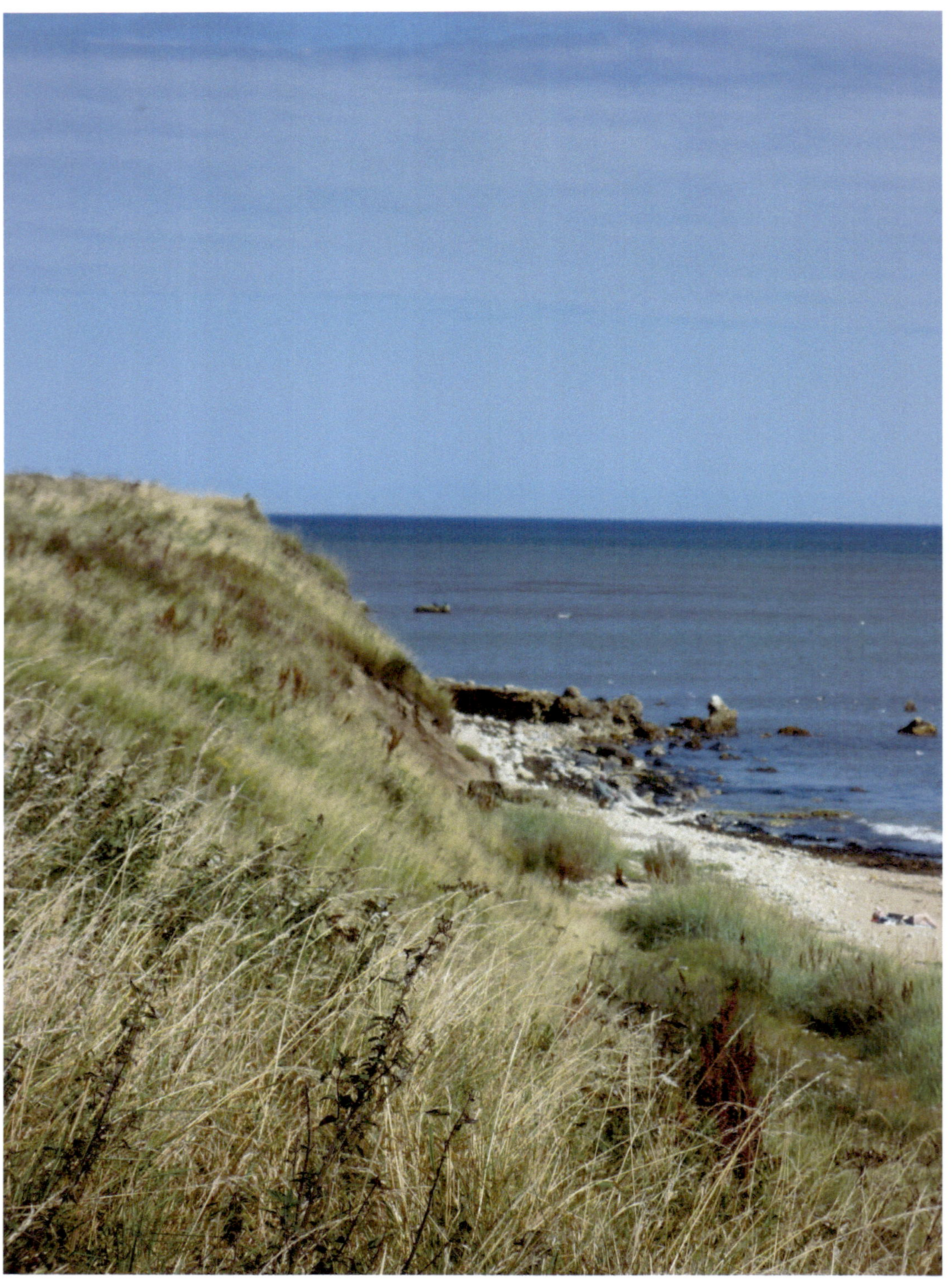

One of the many beautiful beaches.

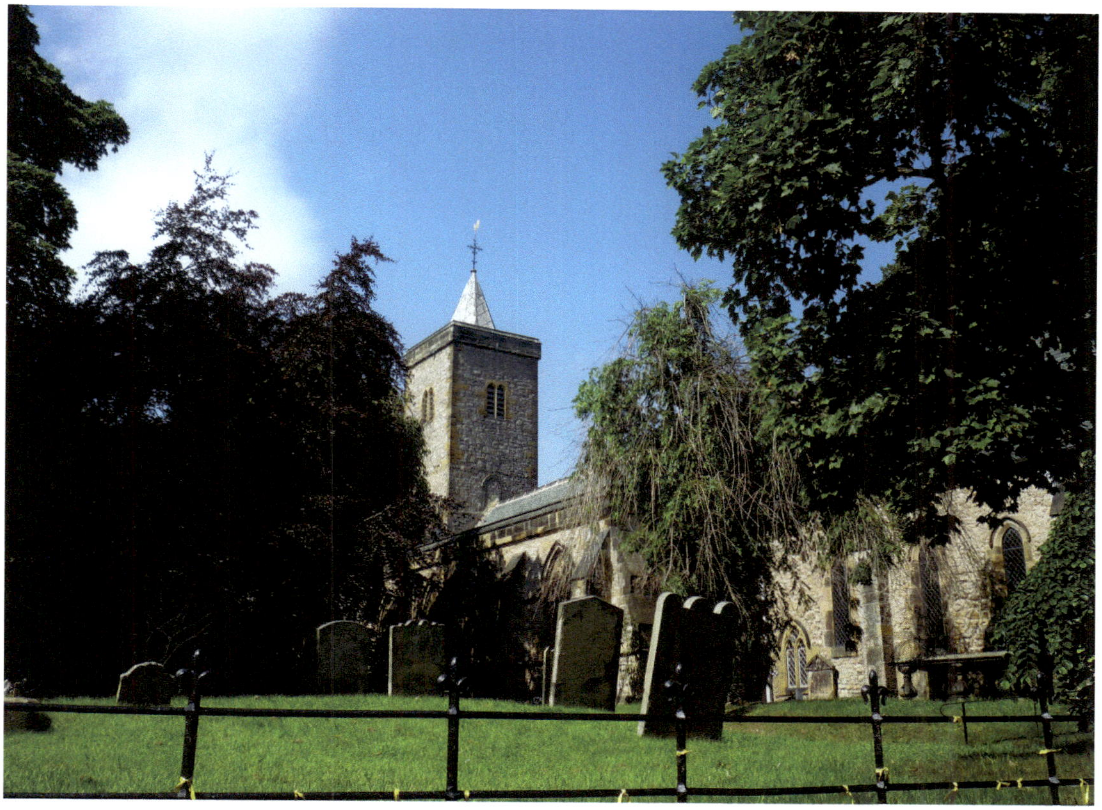

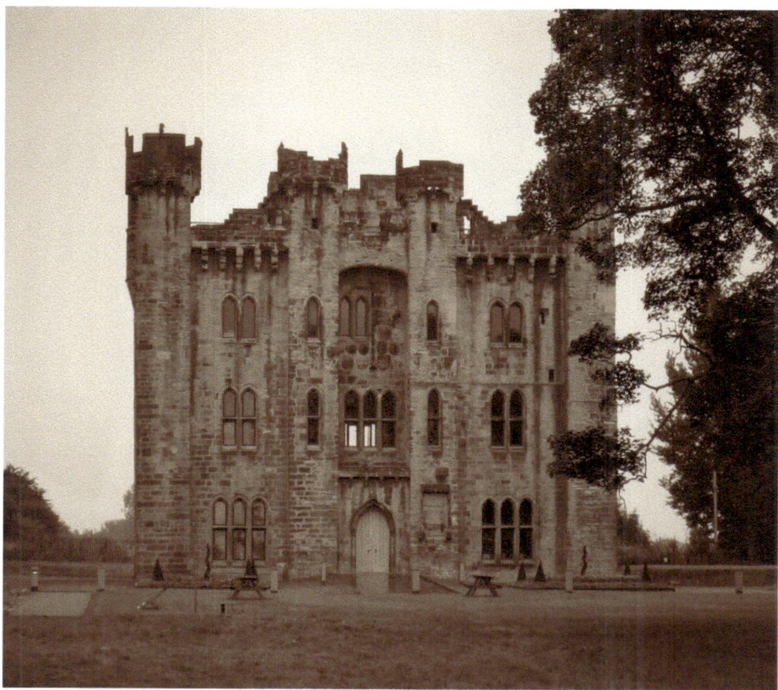

Above: Whitburn Church.

Right: The most haunted building in Sunderland?

CHAPTER 1

Queen's Street Masonic Lodge

From the outside this looks like a normal building and you would be forgiven for at first thinking it is a small, innocuous place surrounded by a large car park. However, the Phoenix Hall on Queen's Street is the oldest working, purpose-built Masonic lodge in the world and dates back to 1785. If this was not enough for you to be intrigued, the basement of this TARDIS-like building is home to a twelfth-century house – a home that dates back to the original fishing folk of 'Sunder-Land'.

The hall was originally built on a bowling green in an area of Sunderland that was dominated by shipbuilding. It was built in 1785 by the Phoenix Lodge, whose original hall had burnt down two years earlier. The Phoenix Lodge is still active within the hall to this day.

The temple still has the original furniture dating back to it's opening. Ironically, the majority of its fittings came from Newcastle and the Grandmaster's chair has a Newcastle crest on it, showing that there was no rivalry back then. The temple still has the original flooring of black-and-white, chequered tiles with a 'G' in the centre of the ceiling. It is an absolutely wonderful room, full of over 200 years of history of the Freemasons and one of the oldest buildings in the oldest part of Sunderland.

In 1890, the masons bought the house next door and converted it into the dining room with a kitchen installed in the basement, so meals could be cooked on-site. An extension was built in 1923 and provided the hall with a new entrance and a flat for a caretaker (the flat is used as offices today and is entered through a small staircase). In 1990, the masons decided to extend the dining room and at the same time the building was listed as a Grade I listed building.

Today the hall is still used by the various local lodges, but is also earmarked to become a heritage centre for Freemasonry, helping to promote the openness being encouraged by the organisation. The hall is now run by the Queen Street Heritage Trust, a group set up to raise funds and awareness of this fantastic building.

As you walk down a very narrow eighteenth-century staircase into the kitchen area in the basement, there is a small doorway that leads you into a dark cellar area and when the light is switched on you are standing in a house dating back nearly 1,000 years. It is a large one-floor building, which has obviously had its roof removed to build the hall above. The walls are made of large stones, but you can still see where the windows and door would have been. Dotted around the room are a number of small pits that have been dug by archeologists. The area is believed to date back to the twelfth century, which has been verified by some of the finds discovered during the digs (some of the items are displayed upstairs in the dining room). One of the items found was a leather shoe. This was found under the doorway. The shoe has been tested and dates back to twelfth century. In years gone by it was thought to bring good luck to place a shoe at the doorway of a new home.

Many other artifacts were found too, from animal bones to clay pots and pipes. All of these items date from throughout the centuries of the past 900 years. As if this was not enough history lying under one building, one of the digs discovered something quite extraordinary that may lead us to believe it could also be the site of a building that seems to be a bit of a mystery in Sunderland.

On the north of the Wear sits the church of St Peter's. It is believed that the church of St Paul's was built on the south side of the river, but no one knows exactly where it was placed. During one of the digs below the Phoenix Hall, the archeologists discovered an incredibly old medieval drainage system. Where the drainage system leads to is still a mystery. Common sense leads us to think it must end at the river somewhere due to the close proximity of the building; however, back then a normal dwelling would not have had that sort of luxury. Indeed, the only place that would have a drainage system that complex would have been a building of importance – such as a church.

Is this the area where the mysterious St Paul's Church of Sunderland once stood? The area would seem to be right, as Hendon is one of the oldest parts of Sunderland and indeed is surrounded by buildings and landscapes of days gone by. Hopefully, one day this question will be answered by the Queen Street Heritage Trust's further investigations.

Ghost stories around the building are unsurprising due to its age, and I have been told a number of them over the years. The one that is often repeated is the story of a man that stands at the bottom of the staircase to the building. He is described as a large man dressed in Victorian clothing. He stares up the stairwell at the people coming down and then disappears. Voices are also often heard coming from the basement and the underground croft. When the area is checked, there is nobody in the building. I was lucky enough to visit the building on a number of occasions to conduct paranormal investigations and can verify the stories of the voices coming from below ground level.

One of the most unusual events in the building did actually happen in the basement, near the doorway to the twelfth-century house. It was a warm summer's evening and we had gathered in the dining hall area when we heard a noise from downstairs and what we thought were voices. There was a group of eight of us and we were all accounted for. As a group, we went downstairs to see who was down there. Nobody was found, so we walked through the basement, towards the entrance to the underground house, where the group stopped. On the floor in front of us was a wet patch and, as you can see in the photographs, it was in shape of two perfect footprints. The floor in the entire building was bone dry. It was a summer evening and we hadn't had rain for several days. We had no explanation for the wet floor, never mind the fact that they were footprints. We later returned to the area and the footprints had gone, dried up, and no water was found in the area.

The twelfth-century house is home to many reports of figures that are seen moving in the darkness. I was with a group of people underground when two people said they had seen a dark figure in the corner of the room, which they thought had been that of a child or small adult. When we looked in the corner from across the room it did appear that a small figure was crouched down. The video footage that was taken at the time showed a dark blur in the same area, but it wasn't as clear as it was to the naked eye. When we approached the shadow it disappeared, and the blur on the screen vanished at the same time.

A building with so many years of history must have its fair share of stories to tell, and I must say that the Phoenix Hall is one of the most interesting buildings I have visited on Wearside and is a true hidden gem.

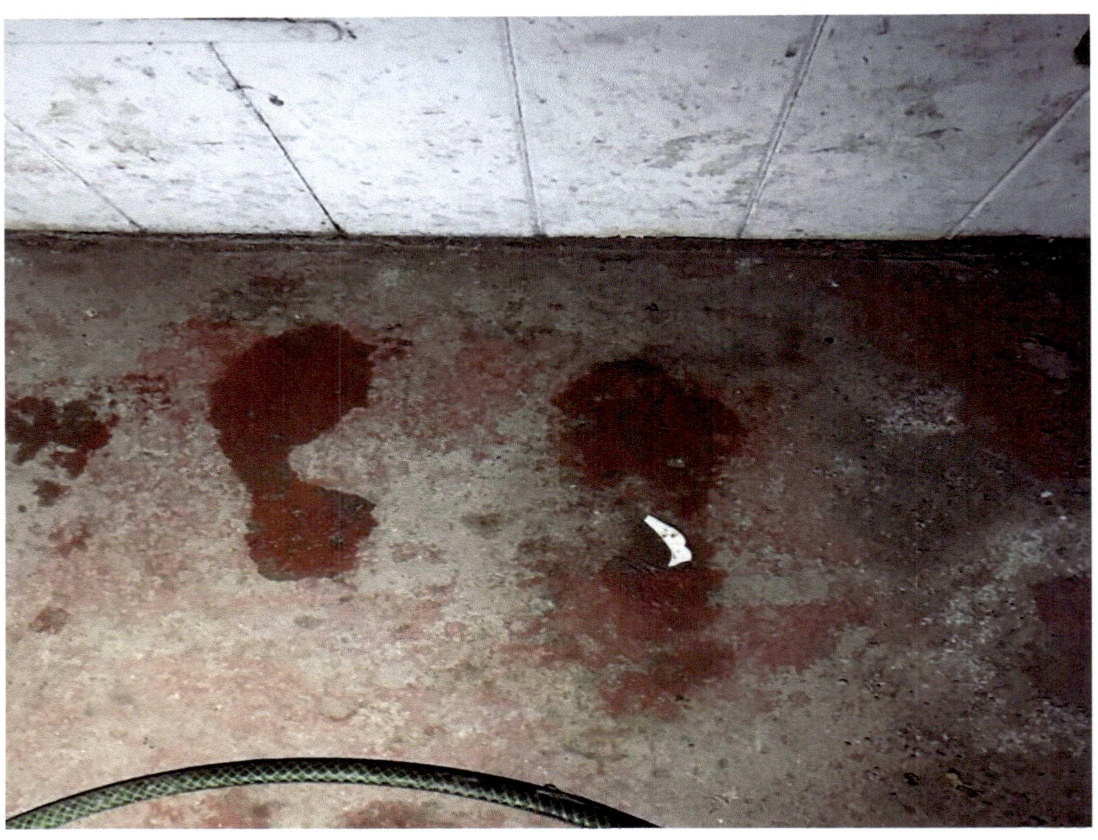

Wet footprints found in the basement that we can't explain.

CHAPTER 2

North East Land, Air and Sea Museum

The North East Air Museum has recently been renamed as the North East Land Sea and Air Museum (NELSAM) and is situated right next door to Nissan on the outskirts of Sunderland, bordering onto the nearby town of Washington. Its proximity to the Nissan site will become more intriguing as we look at the history of the site.

In October 1916, the first aeroplanes took off from what would become known as RAF Usworth. Originally a flight station known as Hylton, it was home to part of the Flying Corps, who were used as part of the home defence to protect the country against attack during the First World War.

After the war the area was unused and fell into disrepair for over a decade. It wasn't until 1932 that it reopened as an airfield, remaining in operation until 1939. In 1939, a concrete runway was laid to replace the field that had been used over the past twenty years.

As the Second World War began the airfield was used by various squadrons, including a visit from the now famous Spitfires. Although no attack on home soil was recorded, two major accidents occurred during training in 1940: one on 26 June and the second on 9 September. Sadly, both led to the deaths of the pilots involved. At the end of the war the airfield once again was not used for flying planes: until 1952 it was used as a storage area for the RAF.

In July 1964, the Sunderland Corporation bought the airfield and reopened the site as Sunderland Airport. It would become the home of Sunderland's Flying Club a year later, after new runways were laid.

In 1974, a group of volunteers started to meet at the airfield and began purchasing old aeroplanes for what was to become the North East Air Museum. But in 1984 it was announced that the airport was to make way for the Nissan Car Plant. Over the following twelve months the future of the museum hung in the balance until a deal was struck to rehouse the exhibits on a site north of the runway.

The museum now houses numerous artefacts from the past century, including some of the finest examples of planes and helicopters and now (recently added) vehicles.

One further point of interest is that the site is reportedly built on a Roman or Dark Age settlement. Notable archaeological digs should have taken place before the building of Nissan's site, but this has always been denied by Sunderland Council and the car company, although two skeletons were discovered on the NEAM site when they were being rehoused.

Paranormal activity has been reported many, many times here over the past thirty years. In fact, the number of reports led the TV programme *Most Haunted* to broadcast an episode in one of its first series. During the programme there are many reports of things being seen and unexplained noises and movements around certain vehicles throughout the various hangars.

Stories have been told of spirits still connected to not only the land around the museum, but also revisiting their much-loved aeroplanes. The most famous and easily researched story is one of a pilot who died in a flying accident near the hangars. He is said to be looking for his boots, which were unfortunately lost in the field where he died. On many occasions the dark figure of an airman in a uniform and hat has been seen walking around the hangar. Footsteps are often heard in the same area and are described as sounding odd – perhaps due to it being the sound of only one boot.

Another story is of a German spy who was captured during the Second World War. He is believed to be Czechoslovakian and was sent to England by the Nazis. It is said that he still bangs and clatters around the hangar as he is trying to escape England to return home, still remaining angry at being caught. I have been present in this hangar when a multitude of unexplained noises came from around it. At first the noises were metallic, as if someone were throwing nails or screws at the corrugated metal walls. Whispers followed these noises, although we couldn't understand what was being said. The noises became more intense when one of the team called out in German, and the banging on the walls became louder and more frequent.

NELSAM produced one of the strangest photographs I have taken during my time as ghost hunter. The picture was taken during the daytime in the main hangar. I wasn't taking photographs for paranormal reasons; I was there looking at the museum and the aeroplanes. My wife had taken a seat, so I took a few photos of where she was sat. After getting home and looking through the photos on the computer I discovered an unusual mist over her head coming from the plane behind her. I had taken over a dozen pictures of this area and this was the only one with this anomaly. When we returned a few weeks later I took photographs in the same area and the mist was not there this time. However, much to my surprise, I found a second photo from a different part of the hangar that also had a mist – this time looking like a hand over the lens.

The newest part of the museum is the new transport area. This area includes buses, coaches, and trams. The black Blackpool tram was the centre of unexplained activity for an entire group of over twenty people, none of whom can explain what we experienced.

We were conducting a public ghost hunt and the group gathered on the lower deck of the tram. We started to call out and ask questions about the history of the tram. We all went silent when we heard footsteps from above. We called out again and it sounded like the footsteps had walked to the top of the stairs. The silence was broken when the sound of a bell was heard from the front of the tram. There was nobody else in the building with us, never mind in the actual tram. Some of the group went upstairs as they were convinced someone must be there, but no one was found. We also checked the bell in the cab of the tram: it didn't work. To this day we still have no explanation as to what could have caused these noises. When I spoke to the gentleman who works at the museum, he said that this had been reported before and there was a belief that the tram had been involved in a fatality during the 1950s, although there are no records confirming this.

With so many historic items and a history of its own, it is no wonder that NELSAM is thought to be one of the most haunted locations in Sunderland. I can confirm that on my many visits and the stories I have been told, this may not be far from the truth.

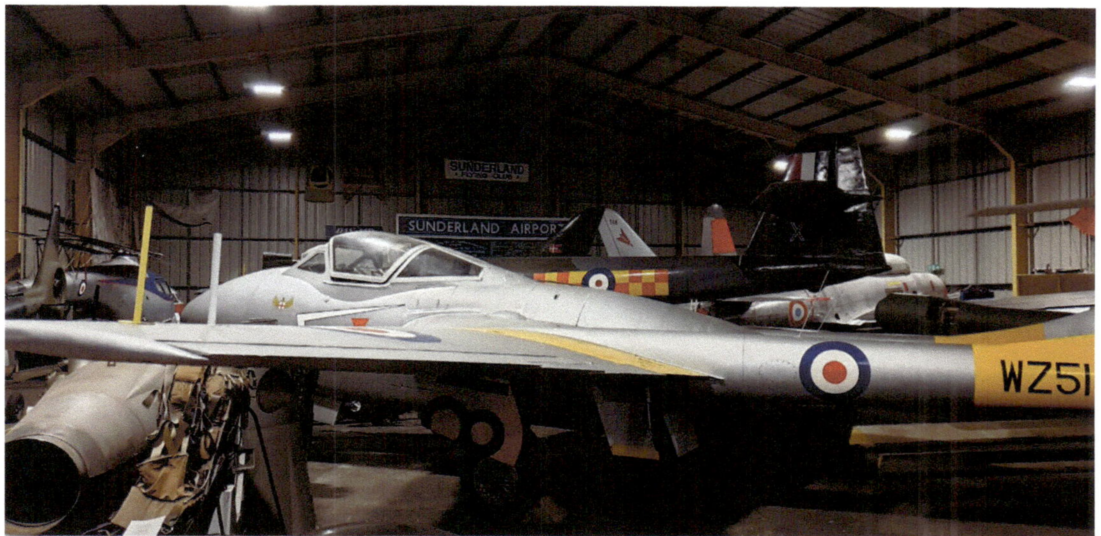

Inside the main hangar.

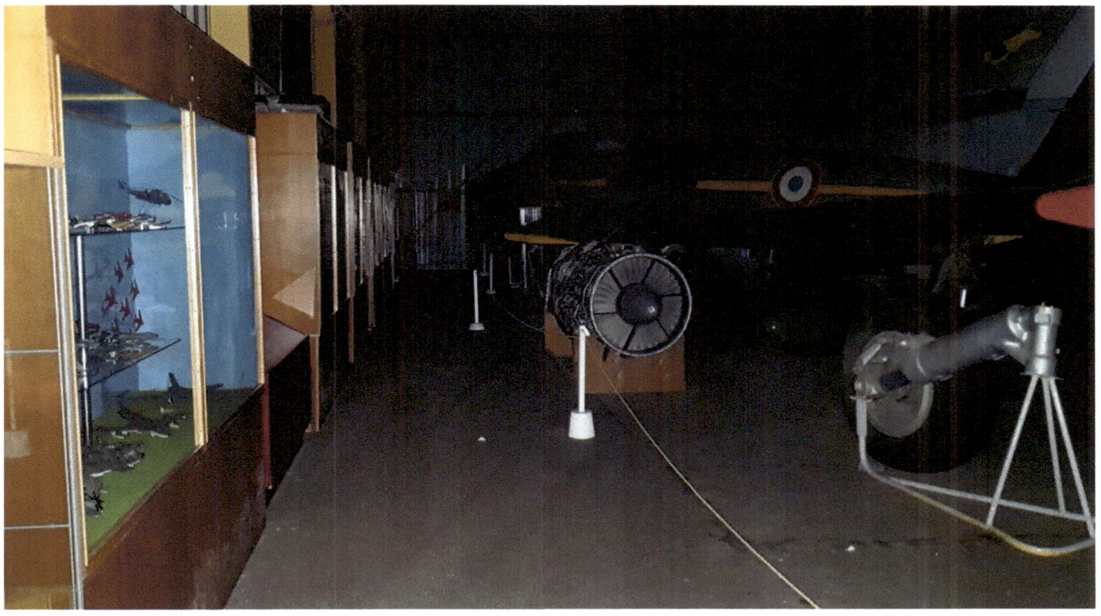

The area where a dark figure and footsteps are heard.

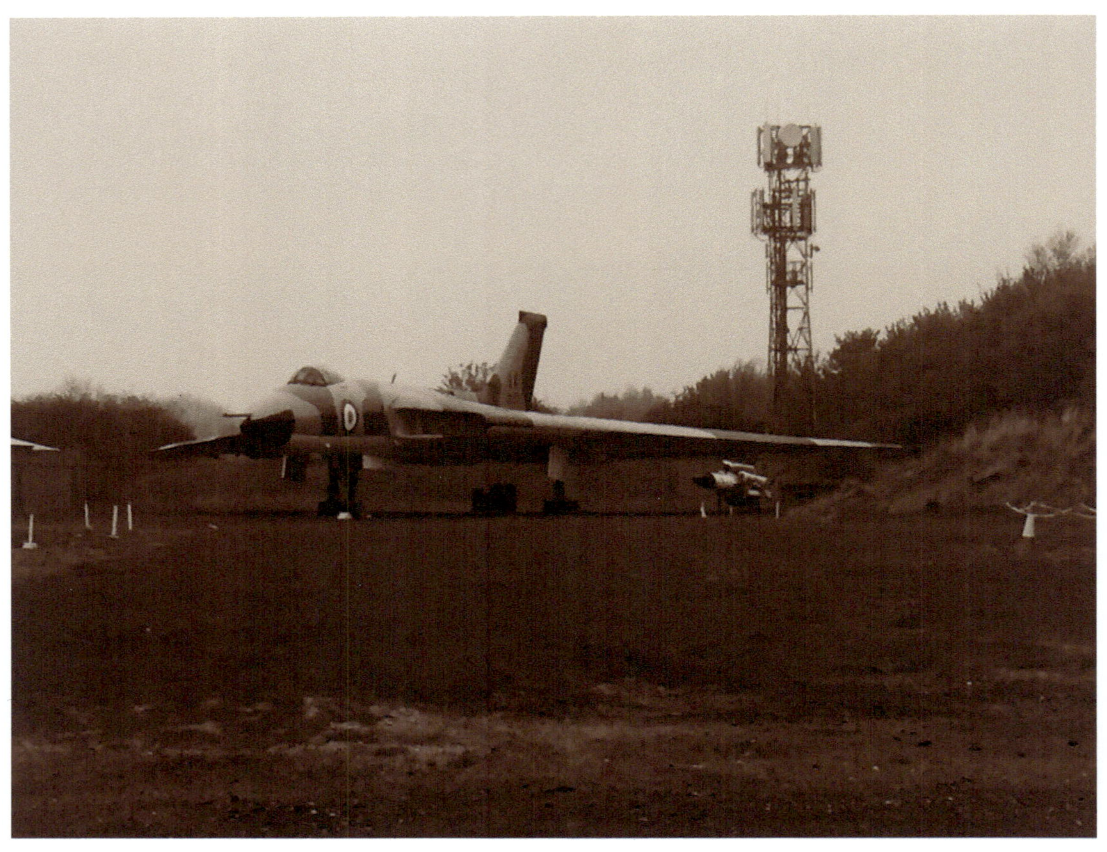

The restored Vulcan Bomber on display outside the museum.

CHAPTER 3

Seaton Holme, Easington

Located on the outskirts of Sunderland you will find Easington, which is split in two: the large Easington Colliery to the east and the smaller parish of Easington village to the west. Seaton Holme sits in the middle of Easington village, opposite the twelfth-century St Mary the Virgin Church and its history is vast with many stories that link the building with Pagan burial grounds, popes, Alice in Wonderland and the Queen Mother to name but a few.

Just when it is thought that the history of the area has been written, more information is found that lets us know just how far back in time the village goes.

A Pagan burial mound was found in the village and is believed to date back as far as the sixth century; certainly, some of the artifacts in the twelfth-century church suggest some form of settlement during the eighth century.

Easington is mentioned in writings in the 900s, with Seaton Holme believed to have been built on a previous structure. The village was an affluent area during the Middle Ages as it became central to the bishops of Durham, although it would be hit by the Black Death and the Border Wars during this time. It continued to be important, however, as it was used as a stopping point for stagecoaches and the postal services during the seventeenth and eighteenth centuries.

During the nineteenth and twentieth centuries the adjoining town of Easington Colliery became a major player in the British coalfields. However, the decline of the pits in the 1980s saw the colliery close down and the town suffer from mass unemployment. Unfortunately, Easington hasn't been able to find a way to return to its former glory as of yet.

We know that a building stood on the site of Seaton Holme during the late Anglo-Saxon period, but the building that we see today dates back to around 1240, although obviously this has had many alterations. It was described as a manor house and was used as rectory to the bishops of Durham until 1832.

It is believed that the church and rectory were home to some important people as they mastered their trade, and the records mention Nicholas Breakspear who would become Pope Adrian IV in the twelfth century – the first from England. Another pope mentioned is Robert of Geneva, who would become Pope Clement VII in 1378. These are just two names that stand out in a list of high-ranking members of the Church.

Jumping forward in time, and after several alterations to the building, we can see through the records that in the 1790s Seaton Holme is listed as a rectory with seventeen rooms. In 1832, Seaton Holme was to house one of its most famous rectors: Revd Henry Liddell. Liddell had married Charlotte Lyon. Their line would marry into the Bowes family, creating the Bowes-Lyons, who are direct ancestors of HRH the Queen Mother.

Liddell's granddaughter would also inspire one of the world's best-known children's stories, *Alice's Adventures in Wonderland*. The reverend's son, Henry George, was close friends with Lewis Carroll, and Carroll spent a lot of time with the family. The character Alice in the book is based around Alice Liddell and the story was inspired from tales he used to tell the children on days out. Over the coming fifty years Seaton Holme would change hands and uses.

In 1921, the building was bought by the Guardians of the Poor. They used the building for the next decade as a children's home, housing the young that were employed by the nearby workhouse. This changed in 1931, with it becoming a hostel for poor and ill men. After the Second World War the county council took over the building to use as a community space, but the building fell into decline and was too dangerous to inhabit, so the decision was made to close it down.

The Seaton Holme that had once been a majestic rectory and manor house was now a dilapidated, empty shell. Thankfully, in 1988 the building was bought by Easington Parish Council for £1. After fundraising and much help from the community, they have rebuilt it back to its former glory and it is now a central hub for many activities. Seaton Holme is now a Grade I listed building and can boast of being one of the oldest domestic buildings in the world.

There are a number of ghost stories surrounding Easington village; for example, the many reports of figures seen in St Mary's Church graveyard, or tales of the ghosts of two men hanged on the village green for trying to put Mary, Queen of Scots on the throne. But the most famous is that of the Easington hare.

As legend has it, a group of hunters were constantly harassed by a hare when they went out hunting, but it always mysteriously managed to evade capture. On one night one of their dogs managed to bite the hare's leg and the group chased the trail of blood. The trail led to a small cottage and, as they burst in, they were left aghast at the sight of an old woman lying on the floor bleeding from her leg. The woman was branded a witch. She was allowed to stay in the village, but was shunned by villagers until she died. Her body was then buried in the churchyard in consecrated ground.

Seaton Holmes' stories mostly revolve around the sightings of priests and dark, shrouded figures seen in and around Seaton Holme. During our pre-investigation visit we were to witness some very unusual happenings. Footsteps were heard above us on the stairs and corridor and as all the team were in the room at the time, we could easily rule out anybody being there. In the cellar, two of the team witnessed a shadow coming down the stairs. They shouted out as they thought it was part of the team coming to join them, but no one appeared. This was followed by them reporting giggling coming from the same place, which they said sounded like small children.

We also witnessed something that has been reported by members of staff in the past. While in the upstairs corridor we twice witnessed a large gust of wind. I say wind as it was not a draught and both connecting doors were shut at the time. The room temperature never changed on any of our equipment, even though we all reported the cold that we had felt at the time.

The history of both the village and Seaton Holme is probably the vastest I have had to research. Each story takes you in a different direction and covers anything from witchcraft to the church. We have only visited the building once and it certainly left us shaken up by some of the unexplainable results.

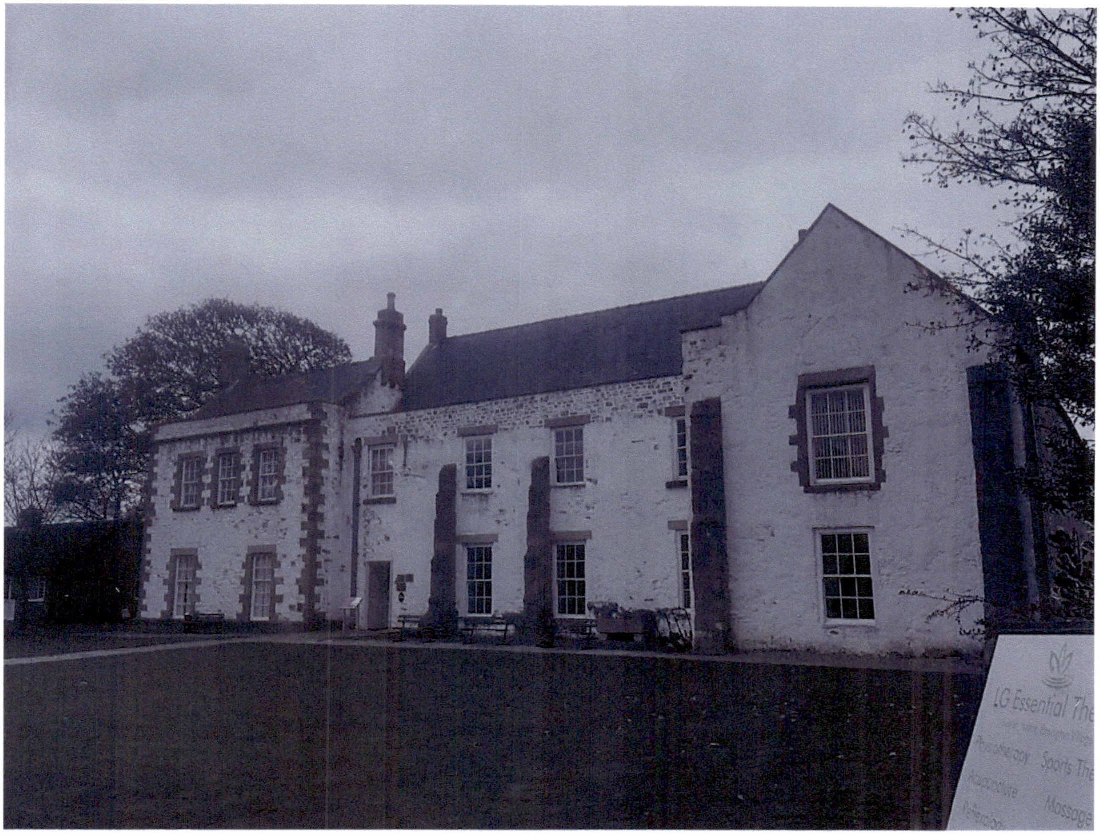

Above: Seaton Holme, built in the thirteenth century.

Right: Under the house is the original cellar said to be the home of several spirits.

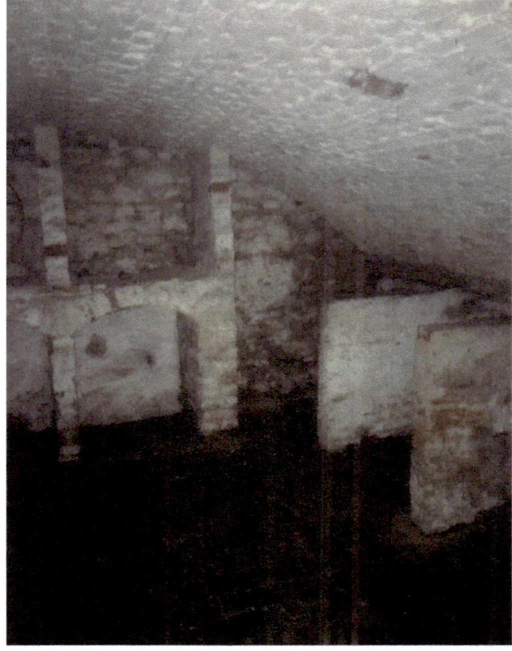

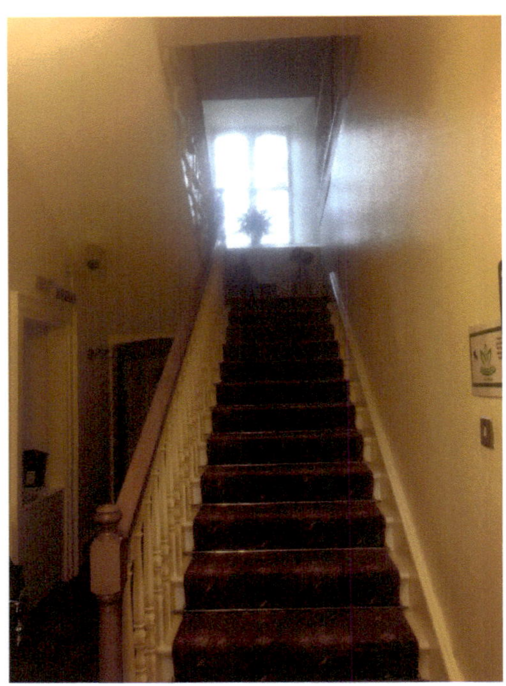

Left: Staircase up to the first floor.

Below: The room where a figure of a man has been seen sat near the fire.

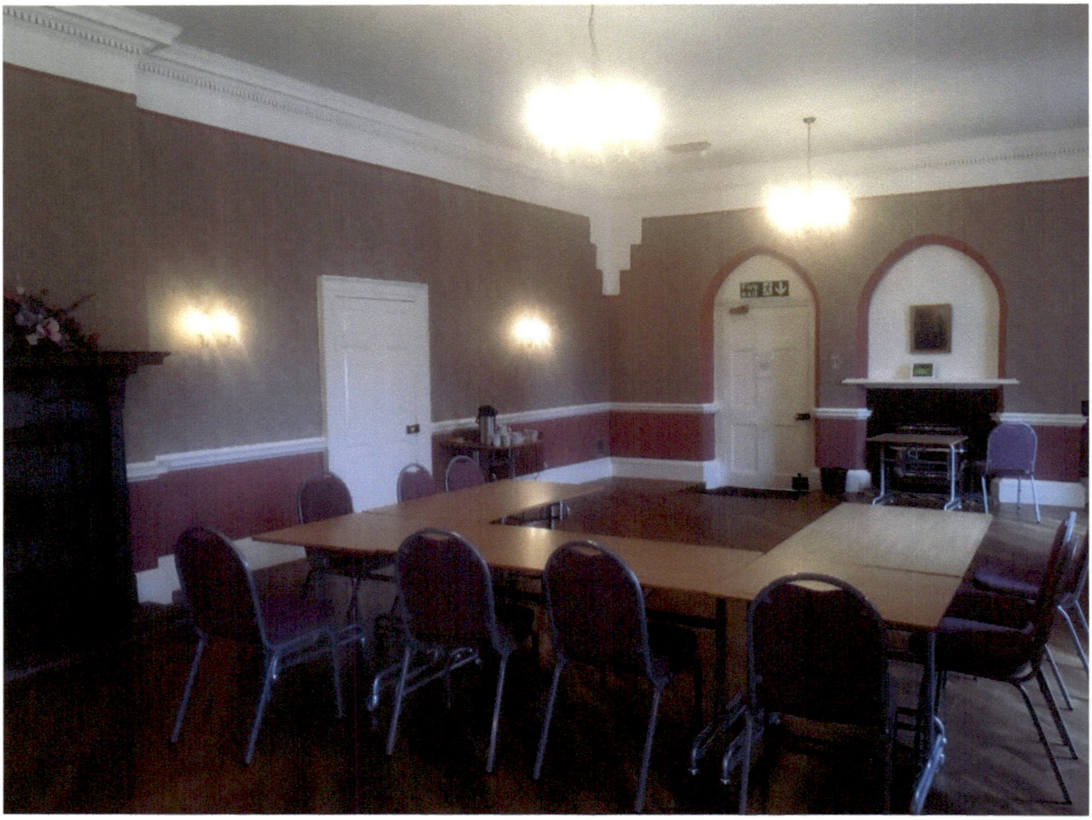

CHAPTER 4

The Royalty Theatre

This fantastic Victorian building just off Chester Road in the heart of Sunderland is the current home for the Sunderland Drama Club and can boast of being Sunderland's oldest community theatre, as the club dates back to 1925.

The building is spread across two floors and has a 250-seat auditorium, a bar, foyer, small theatre and upstairs houses a rehearsal room. The building used to belong to the Union Congregational Church and its original features can be seen throughout, no more so than the auditorium where you can look up and you can still see the beams from the original church.

During the First World War it was used as a military hospital, treating the wounded coming home from battle. During the Second World War a bomb fell outside, only to bounce over the building before exploding, leaving the building untouched.

The drama club have used the Royalty on and off since its beginnings, and in 1969 they bought it outright and have been showcasing its productions ever season since. Coincidentally, my first visit to the theatre to investigate the reports of paranormal activity coincided with the opening of Noel Coward's *Blithe Spirit* – the story of a couple who hire a medium to contact the spirit world.

As with most theatres, the Royalty has its own share of ghost stories, and its very own resident spirit. There have been many reports of a man in the shadows who sits in the auditorium watching the rehearsals, but when he's approached by members of the cast he disappears. No one knows who this person could be. Footsteps, whistling and moaning have all been recorded around the building, with the majority of these noises taking place around the backstage and staircase areas.

I am lucky enough to have investigated the Royalty on several occasions, and I can report a number of strange ghostly goings on. We recorded the slamming of upstairs doors followed by heavy footsteps walking across the floor above us. The footsteps crossed the landing and started down the stairs. We ran out of the room downstairs to see who was making the noise, as we knew we were the only people in the building, to find that no one was there. We ventured upstairs – and I must admit that my heart was pounding in my chest at this moment – to find all the doors were wide open, even though we knew that we had closed all the doors earlier in the evening.

I have observed a series of strange lights and shadows within the downstairs rehearsal rooms. I was present with a group of guests when we all saw the shadow of a child move across the bottom wall of the room. Later in the evening the cries of a child were heard in this room by another group of guests that were present, and we had not mentioned to them what we had witnessed in that area.

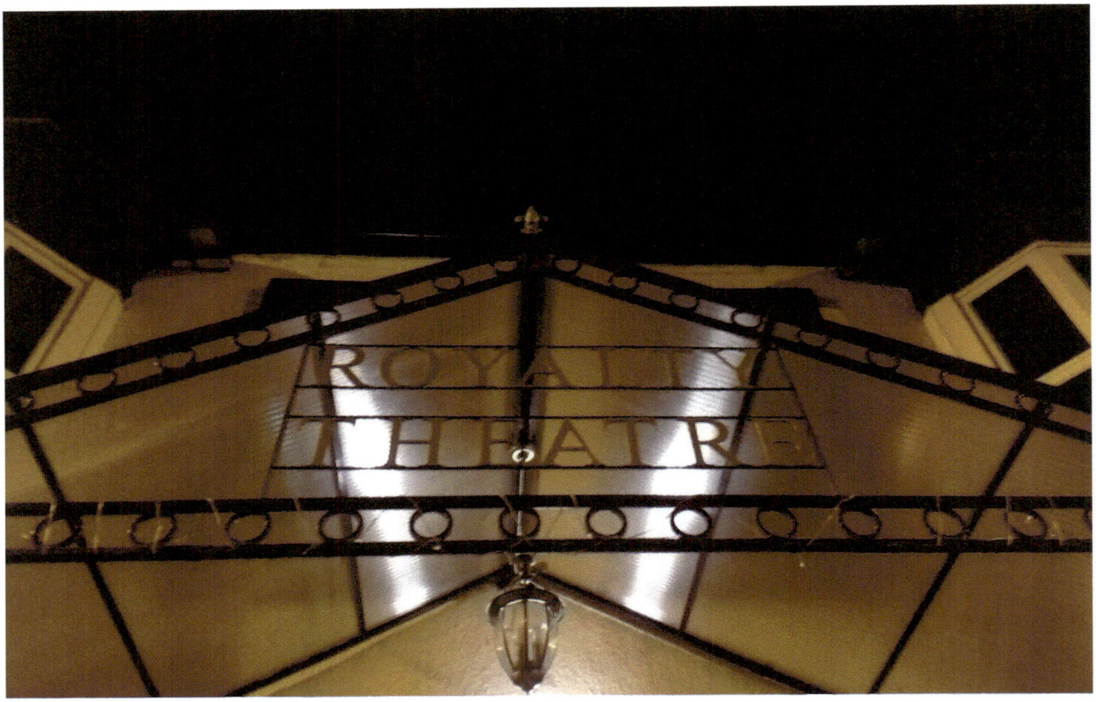

Welcome to the Royalty Theatre.

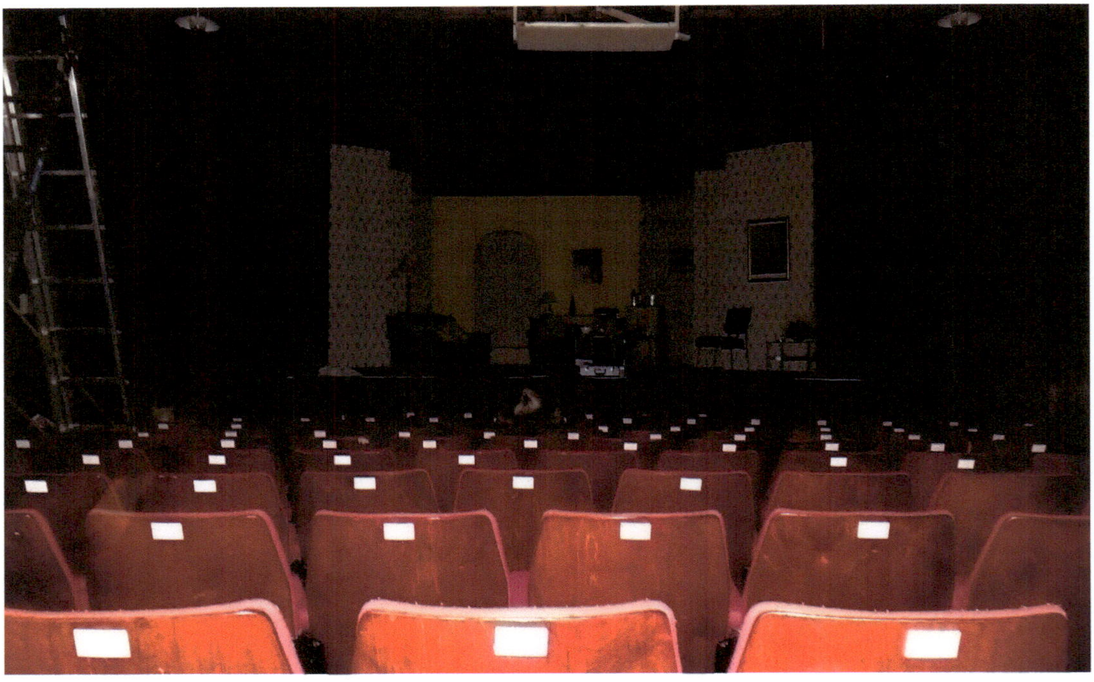

The stage, where many noises are heard.

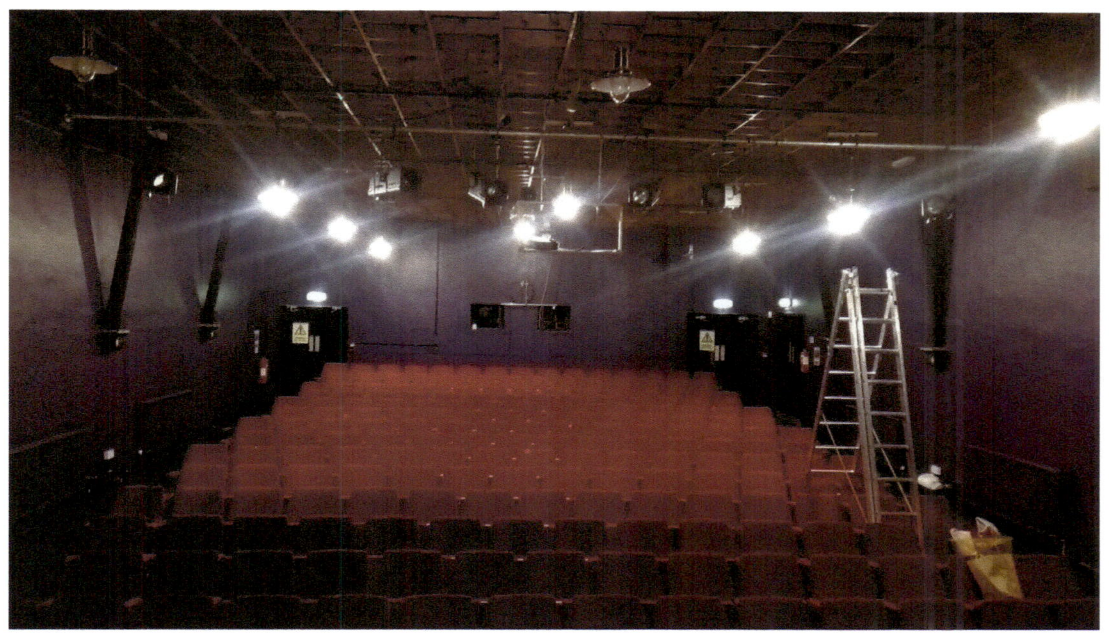

The auditorium, where figures are seen sitting.

However, the most mysterious event I witnessed centred around a camcorder. We placed a camcorder on a tripod in the dressing room and left it facing the door. We switched it on and left for a couple of hours to see what it would pick up. When we returned later in the evening, we found the camcorder had been turned towards the wall. We instantly played the footage back, expecting to see one of the group entering the room, but what we watched left us gobsmacked. On the footage you can clearly hear footsteps walking towards the room; the door doesn't open, but then a few seconds later the tripod is dragged on the floor in 45-degree angle until it faces the wall. I know there was nobody left in the room after the door was shut, and there is no other access into the area apart from the door that stayed shut.

In my experience this extremely historic building will always be one of the most intriguing and spooky places in Sunderland.

CHAPTER 5

Hylton Castle

Hylton Castle is home to probably the best-known ghost story in Wearside: 'The Cauld Lad of Hylton'. But what about the history of this formidable castle nestled on a hill overlooking the Wear?

The Hylton family can be traced back to the ninth century when they were called 'de Hilton'; however, it's not until the late eleventh century when they appear on Wearside. Henry de Hilton fought alongside William the Conqueror during his successful invasion of England and in gratitude the new king gave Henry a large estate of land on Wearside. Henry then proceeded to build the original 'De Hilton Castle'.

The original castle stood for over 200 years and was passed down through the family until the late fourteenth century when Sir William Hylton (it is not known when the family changed its name from de Hilton to Hylton) replaced the original wooden structure with the stone-built manor house that we see now. Over the years the building was expanded with an extension to the north wing and the addition of St Catherine's Chapel.

Over the next few centuries the castle passed through the family, and the castle was altered on numerous occasions by the various sitting Hylton barons. The year 1746 saw the death of John Hylton, the 18th and final Baron Hylton. He died without an heir, so the estate was passed to his nephew, Sir Richard Musgrave. Sir Richard was the 5th Baronet of Hayton Castle and already owned an estate in Cumbria. He decided to sell Hylton Castle in 1749 to Lady Bowes of Streatham and Gibside.

In time, the estate was passed down from Lady Bowes to her grandson John Bowes. John rarely stayed at Hylton, although he did do some substantial work to the castle during his ownership. However, the castle laid empty for many years and started to become ruinous, that is until 1812 when local businessman Simon Temple took ownership. Temple had made his riches from coal mining and had already built the well-known Jarrow Hall, which is 10 miles north of the castle, back in 1785. He started by putting a new roof on the chapel and then made the castle more comfortable to live in; however, Temple's businesses failed and the work he started was never finished due to his bankruptcy.

Over the following century the castle changed hands and was used for various purposes by numerous owners. By the 1950s the castle had become a ruin, along with the chapel. Much of the additional wings had been pulled down due to the structures being dangerous, leaving only the original gate tower that we see today. Thankfully, over the past few years the Hylton Castle Project, alongside English Heritage, have been reviving the castle to its former glory so the public can engage with this 600-year-old building.

After such a long history and boasting to be the second-oldest building in Sunderland, who is 'the Cauld Lad'? For anyone reading this from outside the North East, the word 'cauld' is a slang word for cold. The sighting of this ghost goes back centuries; however, with all folklore there seems to be several versions of the story, but all the stories seem to agree on who the ghost is. The version I'm going to tell is the one that I have been told many times and makes more sense as to why he is 'cauld'.

At the beginning of the seventeenth century the castle was owned by the 13th Baron of Hylton, Robert Hylton. It was said that Robert was not liked by his staff and locals alike. He was a bad-tempered man and only had time for his friends and the ale. One day Robert wanted to go out hunting and went to the stables to gather his horse and equipment. As he entered the stables, he was shocked to find his wife in a very compromising position with a stable boy named Robert Skelton. In a fit of jealous rage, the Baron beat the stable boy to death before dumping his body in a nearby lake.

The history books do indeed show that Robert Hylton was pardoned of murder in 1609, although it does not give us much more detail. Either he was innocent or he managed to pay the right people using his wealth and power.

After this tragic event the reports of ghostly apparitions and strange phenomena started. The ghost is always described as a naked young man that walks the castle saying that he's cauld, so very cauld. When the castle was inhabited it was said he

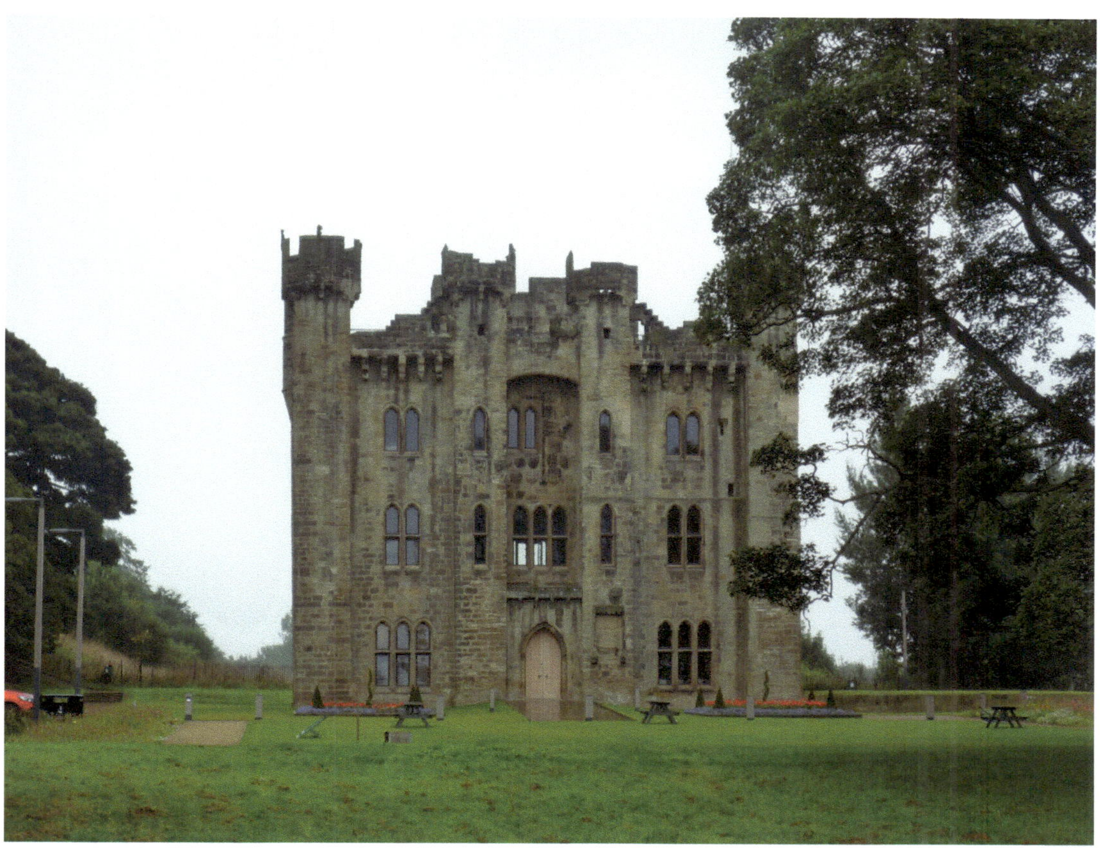

Hylton Castle.

 Paranormal Sunderland

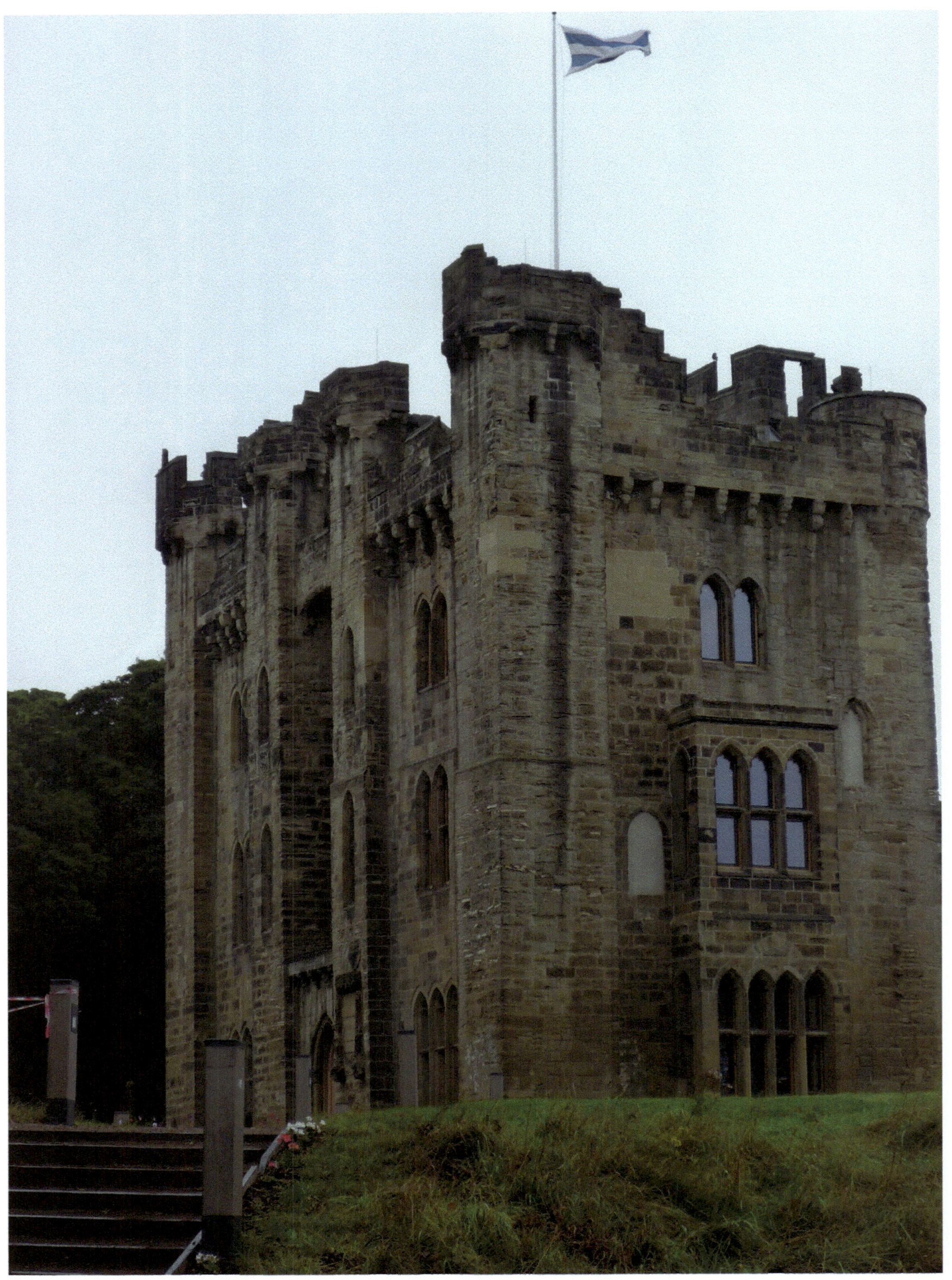

One of the oldest buildings in Sunderland.

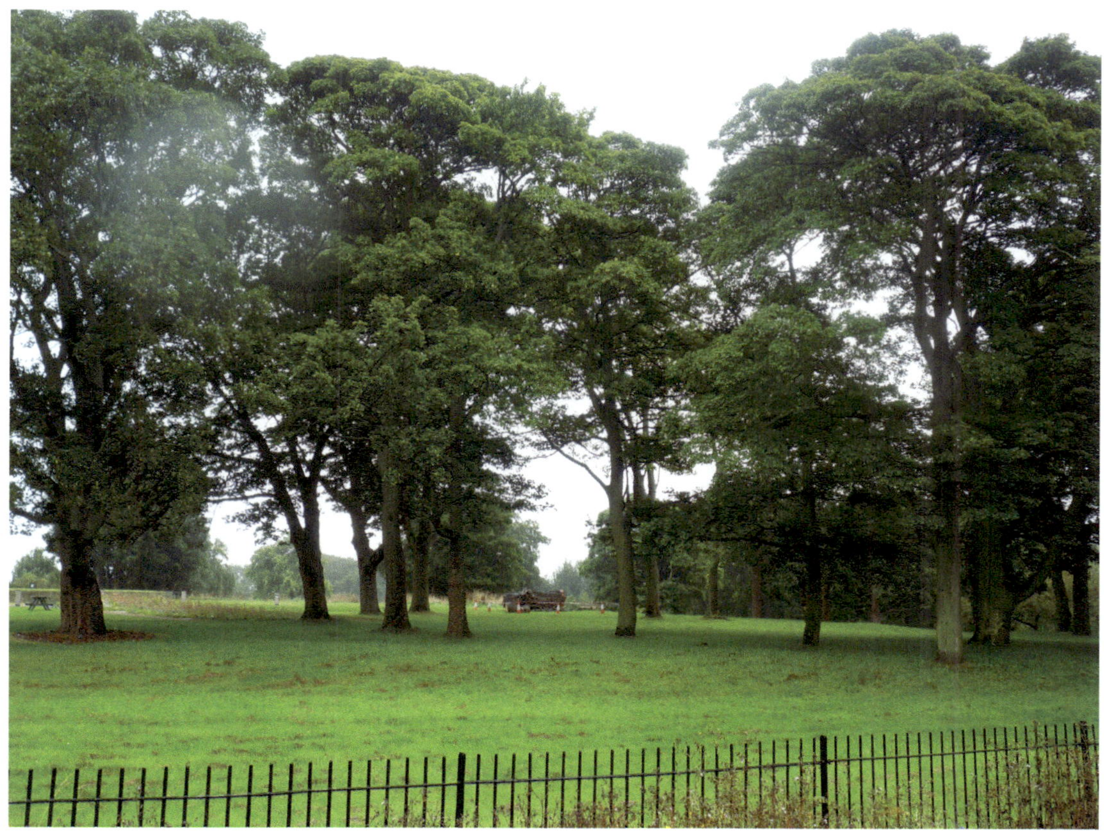

The grounds of the castle.

would push chairs and knock over pans full of hot water and food. Today, he is still reported to walk the castle grounds calling out 'I'm cauld', and it will be interesting to see what shenanigans he will get up to when the castle reopens to the public.

Other stories I have heard over the years include reports of lights being on in the castle even though the building is in ruins. But the lights in the windows disappear when someone gets close enough to investigate.

I was told the story of a gentleman who was walking past when he heard whistles followed by screams coming from the former chapel. He was worried that someone was in trouble and walked up to the ruins, but stopped when he saw several dark shadows float across from the chapel into the castle walls. He said he turned and ran without looking back and never returned to Hylton Castle.

CHAPTER 6

The Barnes Institute, Whitburn

Nestled on the cliffs a couple of miles north of Sunderland is the quaint village of Whitburn, a beautiful, leafy suburb of the now expanded city, which is full of large red-brick houses and buildings that date back to the nineteenth century. There are thoughts that there has been a settlement of some kind here since the Iron Age, but it is not until the twelfth and thirteenth centuries that the village gets any mention of note. We know that the parish church dates back to this time, as some of the original building is included in the church we see now, which was restored during the 1800s.

The church would have sat in the area of Whitburn Hall, which was originally built in the sixteenth century and stood proudly in the village until it was demolished in 1980 after a fire destroyed it. The hall became famous as the home of lawn tennis. The story is that the owners had no courts and on one summer's day they drew a court on the front lawn to play, and that was the birth of lawn version of the sport.

Whitburn is also famous for its links to Lewis Carroll and his Alice in Wonderland books. It is said that Carroll visited Whitburn regularly to stay with family and became friends with Alice's family, the Liddells. It is often stated that he would tell the children wild and wacky stories to keep them entertained, which then became his bestselling stories. Whitburn Beach was the source of inspiration of 'The Walrus and the Carpenter' among others.

Later, as industry changed the landscape, Whitburn changed with it. It became home to the workers of the nearby quarries, brickworks and local Marsden Pit. Thomas Barnes owned the local brickworks and built many of the buildings around Whitburn in the Victorian period. The red-brick buildings that you see today were built using the bricks he manufactured. In 1905, his wife Alice would donate a building to the community, and this is where our first ghost stories of Whitburn will start – at the Barnes Institute.

The Barnes Institute was opened as a community centre, and over the past 116 years it has served the local area well. From its early days it has hosted tea dances, craft classes and an array of community projects. Today it also is home to a large upstairs gym.

I was approached by an ex-employee, who told me stories of doors being slammed, banging from empty rooms and footsteps up and down the stairs. He told me it had been happening for many years, but no one knew why or who could be visiting the building. I've attended the building twice and witnessed some very unusual activity. I was in the large downstairs room when two huge bangs were heard upstairs, which was followed by a door being slammed. As I walked up the stairs I was expecting to see that someone had managed to get past me at the front door. The shivers went down my spine as I searched an empty floor. There was nobody else in the building.

The second time I visited I was upstairs with a group of six. We were trying various paranormal experiments when a loud bang came from above us. This is an empty attic area and we were in the room with the only access point. The banging continued and only 'responded' when we spoke about the war. Unfortunately, we still don't know who the ghost is, but I can assure you that they certainly seem to want to be heard.

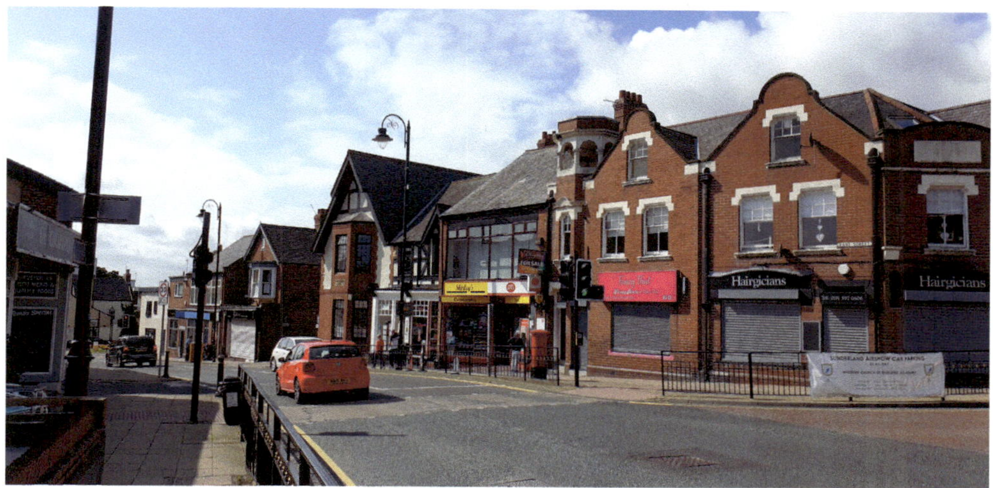

Above: The institute on East Street, Whitburn.

Right: The upstairs corridor, where footsteps are heard.

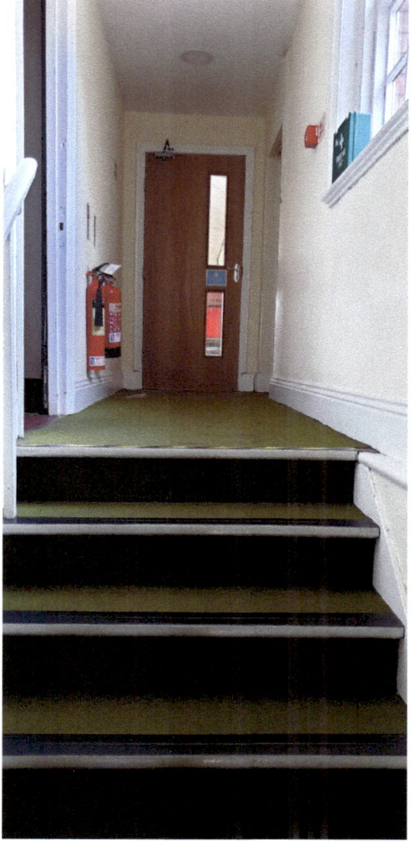

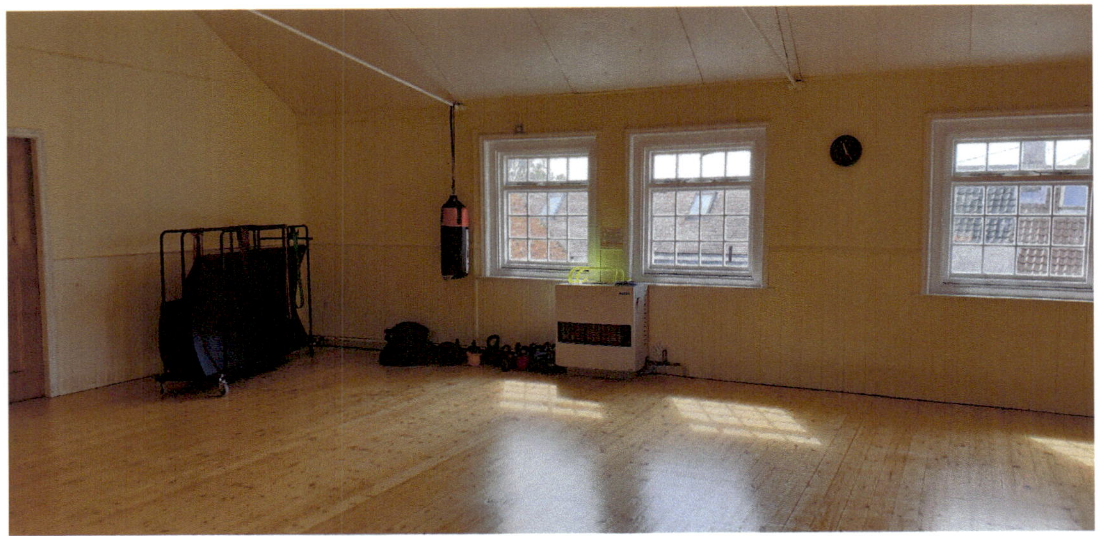

Inside the Barnes Institute.

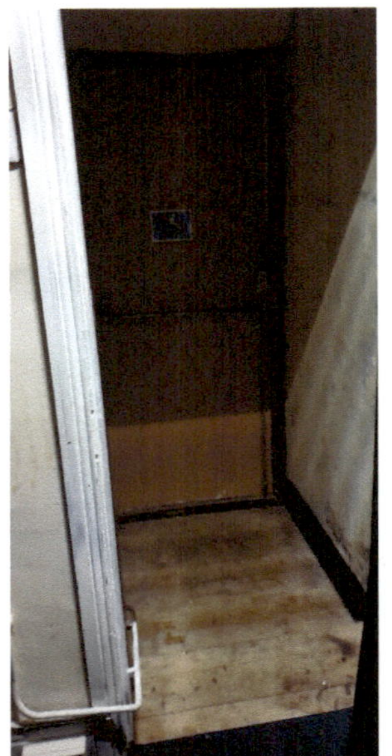

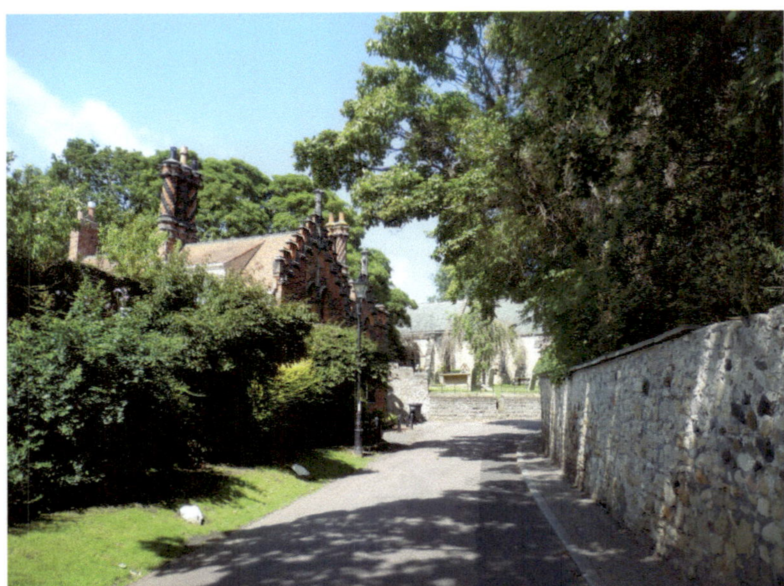

Above left: Banging has been heard from the fire exit.

Above right: Whitburn village.

The Britannia, Cleadon Village

Cleadon is a small village next to Whitburn with a history that dates back over a thousand years. The village pond is believed to be the remnants of a lake from the Ice Age. Located 5 miles north of Sunderland, Cleadon is nestled between the cliffs of the North Sea and the beautiful landscape of the Cleadon Hills. It's believed that there have been settlements around this area dating back to the Neolithic period, when Stone Age humans began to farm the land. The surrounding farmlands would see Cleadon thrive throughout medieval times and beyond, as Cleadon is first mentioned in the Boldon Buke (1183). The Boldon Buke was the first listing of properties that could be taxed by the Bishop of Durham.

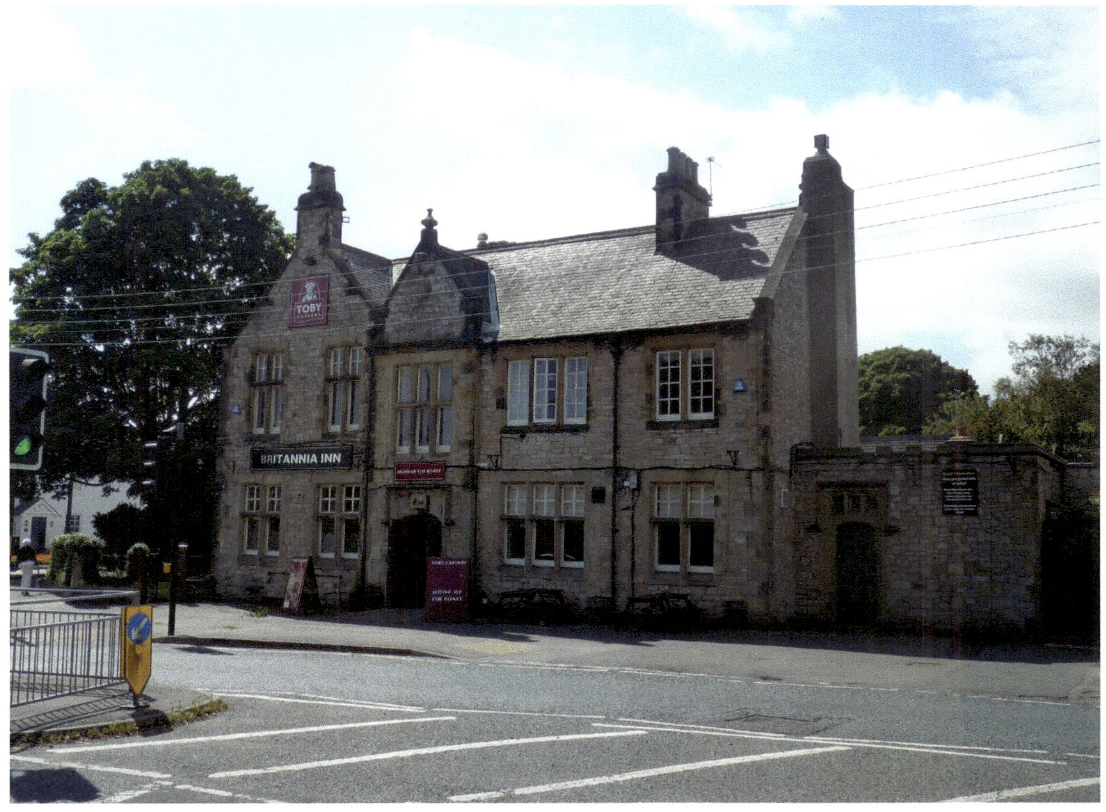

The Britannia Inn, Cleadon.

Over the following centuries Cleadon thrived as a small village due to its farming land and location. During the nineteenth century industry came to the area, as it was quarried for its limestone and later with the manufacture of bricks and ceramics.

Cleadon was well known as a stopping point for travellers between London and Scotland. Its oldest pub is the Britannia, on Front Street, where a coaching inn has stood for the past 300 years. The current building is a Toby Carvery and was built in 1894 on the site of the former coaching lodge. It is home to many ghost stories, including tales of highwaymen, crying ladies and phantom smugglers. With miles of tunnels under the building, linking it to houses and the cliffs, the smuggler stories are unsurprising.

There are many stories that have been written over the years, but the one I have heard several times is about the noise of heavy boots. People had reported hearing the sound of heavy footsteps going up the stairs and along the corridor. It's said that the footsteps are made by heavy boots and are loud. When anyone goes up the stairs to investigate there is no one around, but there is a distinctive smell of rum. Now, it is a pub and always has been, but everyone who witnessed this phenomenon say it is not beer or any other alcohol, it is definitely rum.

Interestingly, the strong smell of rum and tobacco has been reported in the cellar, near to where it is rumoured that the entrance to the tunnels were. In this area the sound of voices and shouting has been heard through the walls. Could it be the ghosts of the smugglers bringing their booty ashore from the boats docked in the bay?

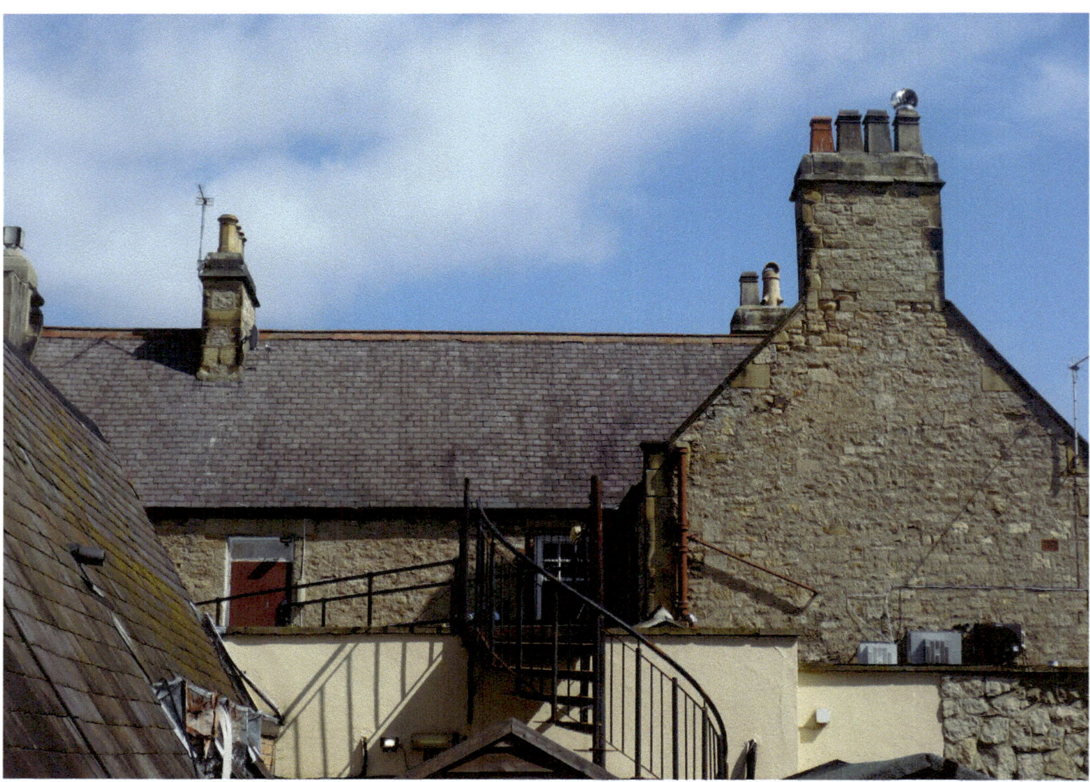

Back of the inn.

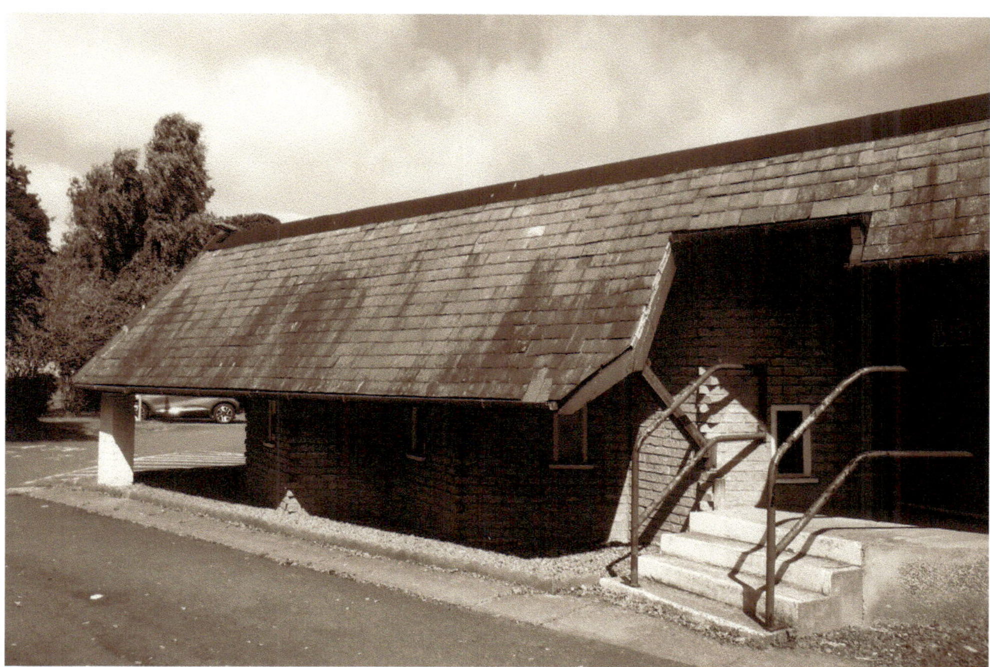

The stable area.

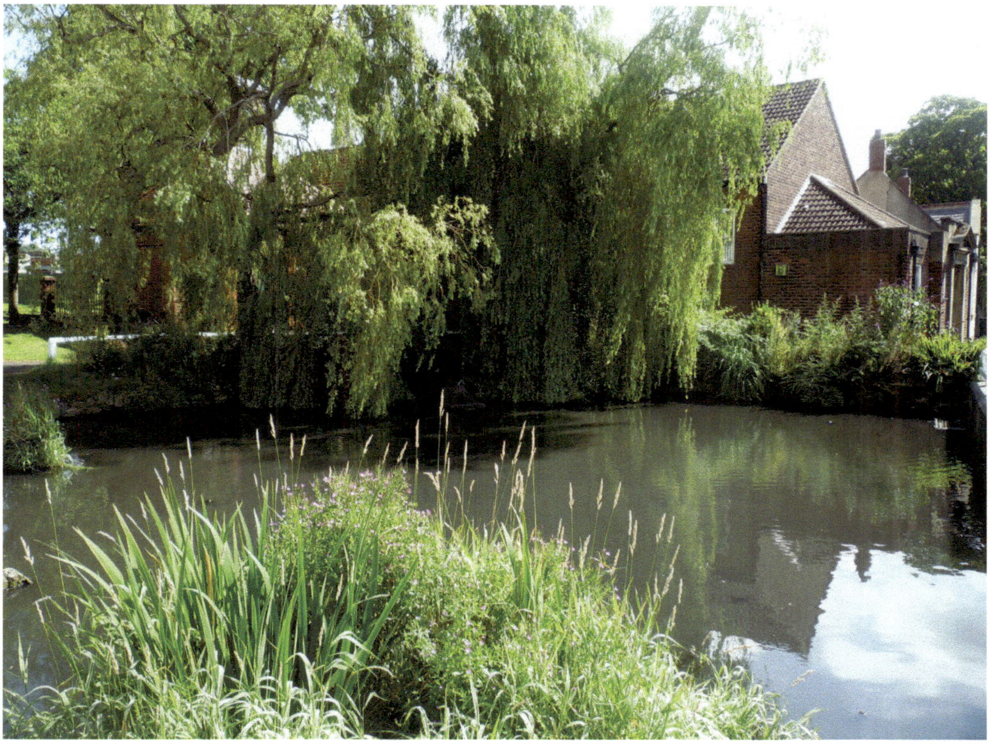

Cleadon village pond, opposite the pub.

CHAPTER 8

Souter Lighthouse

A debate I seemed to get embroiled in when writing this chapter was not whether Souter Lighthouse is haunted, but whether Souter Lighthouse is in Sunderland. People from South Shields and the surrounding area say it is South Tyneside, whereas the Sunderland folk say it's Sunderland. The history books has it listed as Sunderland, South Tyneside and County Durham. However, as it has an SR postcode and has many stories of hauntings, I have included it in the book.

Souter lighthouse was opened in 1871 on Lizard Point, near Sunderland. Originally, the lighthouse was meant to be built a mile down the coastline on Souter Point, but it was relocated due to the clifftops being higher. The name was kept to avoid confusion. The lighthouse was built to protect sailors from what at the time was the most notorious coastline of its day – in 1860 alone there were twenty shipwrecks reported on the reefs just off the coast.

James Douglass designed the iconic red-and-white-striped building, and it became the first lighthouse to be lit by electricity. It's 800,000-candlepower light could be seen for up to 26 miles away. It was in active service until 1988 when it was decommissioned but was still used until 1999 as a radio beacon. Today it is owned by the National Trust and has become a museum where you can look back at the day-to-day life of a lighthouse and its workers.

Just north of the lighthouse is the grassy areas known as the Leas. There once was a village built here called Marsden Village, which had homes for nearly a thousand people. They were to serve the nearby Whitburn Colliery when it opened in 1974. After the colliery closed in the mid-1960s the village was demolished. Although there were many reported tragedies at the mine, there were nearly 100 miners reported to have died in the colliery.

Souter's Lighthouse has featured on television, including on *Most Haunted*, as it is well known for its poltergeist activity. Doors slam around the building, with items being flung around rooms when there is no one there. Full apparitions have been spotted by employees and tourists around the building, while objects regularly go missing only to reappear later in a different location.

The story of the ghost of an old lighthouse keeper has been told many times. It is said that he walks around the lighthouse at both daytime and night-time. He is seen climbing the stairs up to the light and says 'hello' to visitors who are unaware he is a spirit until they speak to the staff and are told that they have nobody in the building wearing a uniform.

A family has been heard in the house that is attached to the lighthouse. At the moment the house is used as a museum and many visitors have reported hearing a family in the rooms, but they are empty when the visitors enter. The staircase is central to the sound of footsteps running up and down, with nobody in the area when the noises are checked.

A personal story I can share is one that left us very confused, but the confusion soon turned to anger. A small group of us were spending the night in the lighthouse to investigate the ghost stories. A friend who was in charge of our video equipment had left us to go around the building and set up the equipment. He soon returned and asked what we had done to the night-vision camera. We all looked at him confused as we did not have any idea what he was referring to. He then explained he had been upstairs and put one of the cameras on the table at the top of the stairs while he took the second camera into one of the rooms. When he returned to the table to set the camera up elsewhere, it had gone. He had looked everywhere for it and returned to us as he thought one of us was playing a trick on him. We explained that no one had left the room we were in. We all then went upstairs to see if we could find the camera. After looking everywhere we could think of, we checked all the doors and window as the only other explanation was that someone had got into the building and stolen it.

Every window and door was locked from the inside. The anger then started as this piece of equipment was worth £500 and not cheap to replace. Later, when we told the site manager, he said it wasn't the first time. Over the years they had many reports of items vanishing with no explanation. He said a builder had been in the building a couple of months earlier and lost some of his tools. To this day, the camera never reappeared.

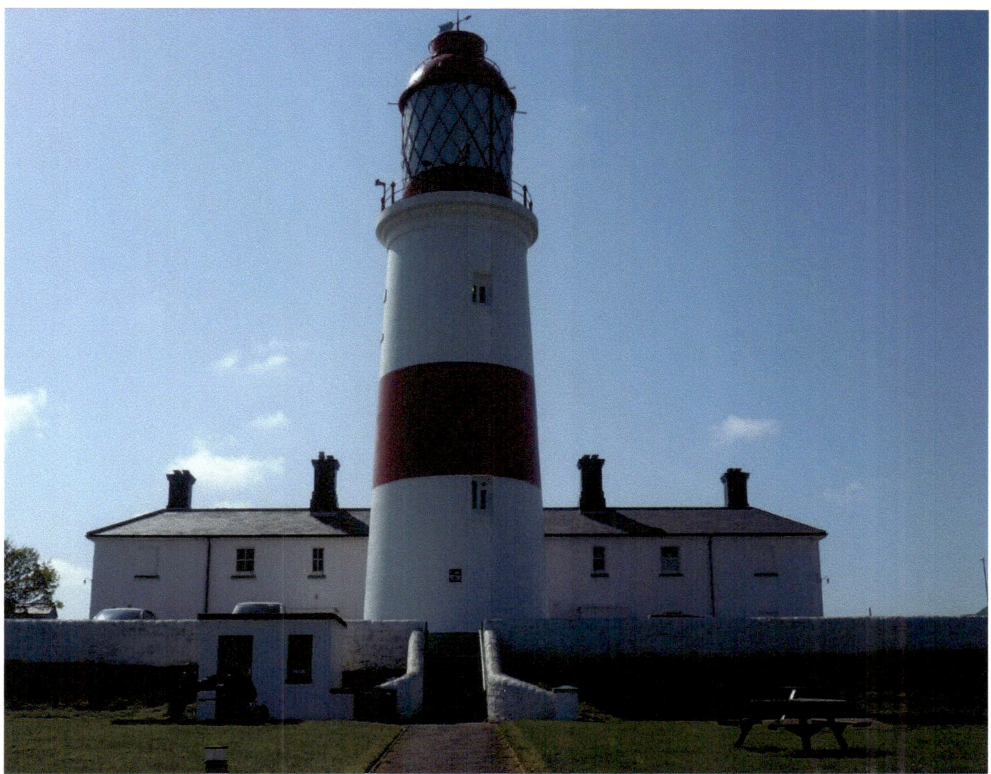

The red-and-white lighthouse still sits proudly on the cliff edge.

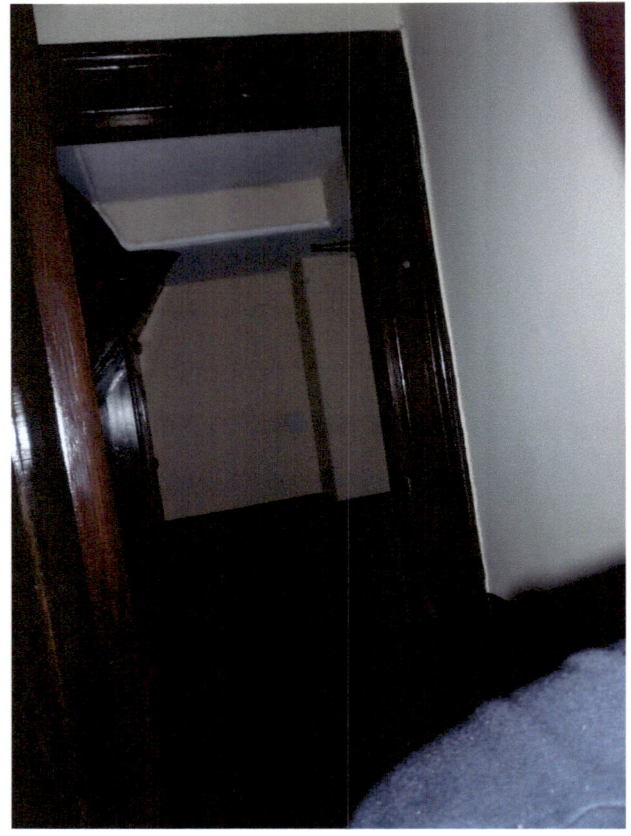

The staircase where people heard walking and talking.

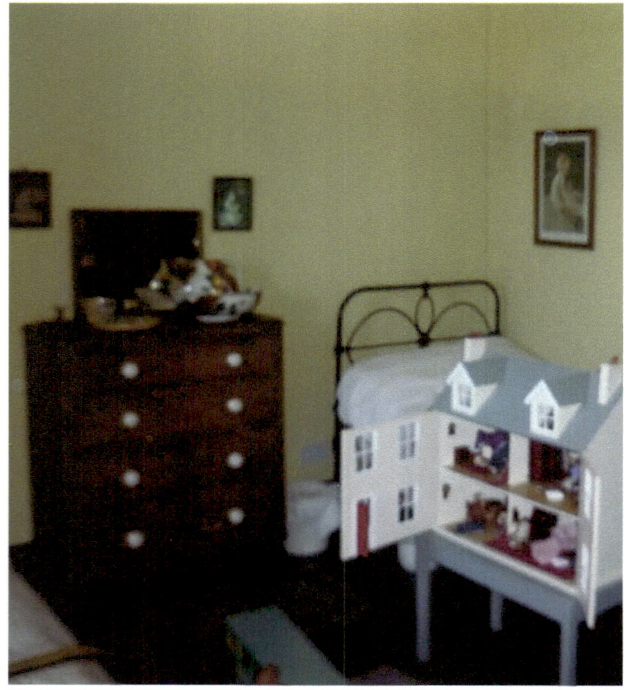

Inside the lighthouse keeper's cottage.

CHAPTER 9

The Empire Theatre

The Emire Theatre opened in 1907 as the Empire Palace, and is the biggest theatre in the North East. Situated in the city centre, like most theatres it has its fair share of resident ghosts. Opened by Vesta Tilley, who had laid the foundation stone nearly a year earlier, the theatre would become a landmark in the city.

During its opening couple of decades, the Empire enjoyed financial success from both local and national shows. However, as the 1930s arrived, the theatre started to see declining audiences and they decided to install a projection camera and screen the latest talkies and then full-colour films.

As the Second World War raged, the theatre saw an increase of audiences flooding back for live performances, but this was only to last for the next two decades and, like most other theatres in the country, by the end of the 1950s audiences had discovered television and the Empire closed its doors. Fortunately, it was only closed for a year. The building was bought by the local council, who saw the importance of keeping this hub of the community open. The theatre has remained open ever since, playing host to some of the biggest London West End travelling shows while still opening its doors for local community production.

The Empire's stage has been home to many household names. The Beatles played the during their first UK tour, Helen Mirren made her stage debut and I think everyone remembers when Hollywood legend Mickey Rooney appeared in panto. But it's the late and great comedy actor Sid James that has left a lasting impression. Sid was one of the most famous actors of the 1960s and became a household name as he was one of the stars of the extremely popular 'Carry On' films before landing the lead role in a TV series called *Bless This House*. His laugh was very distinctive, and he became known for it. On 26 April 1976, he was starring on stage at the Empire in a production of *The Mating Season* when he collapsed due to a heart attack during the performance. Unfortunately, he was pronounced dead on arrival at the Sunderland Royal Hospital.

His ghost is still reported to haunt the Empire to this day. Reports of the sound of his distinctive laughter is often reported behind the scenes. It is heard in his changing room, where actors and actresses have reported feeling his presence while they are getting ready to go on stage. One rumour was that Les Dawson, a well-known comedian of the 1970s and 1980s, stayed in the dressing room as he was appearing in Sunderland. After the first night he asked for a different dressing room and said he would never go back to the theatre again after what he had experienced. Although no one can confirm this story, Mr Dawson never played the Empire again.

A grey lady is often reported in the stalls. The stalls are the highest seats in the house and grey ladies are often reported throughout the theatre community. The grey lady in Sunderland is believed to be Vesta Tilley, the actor who opened the theatre.

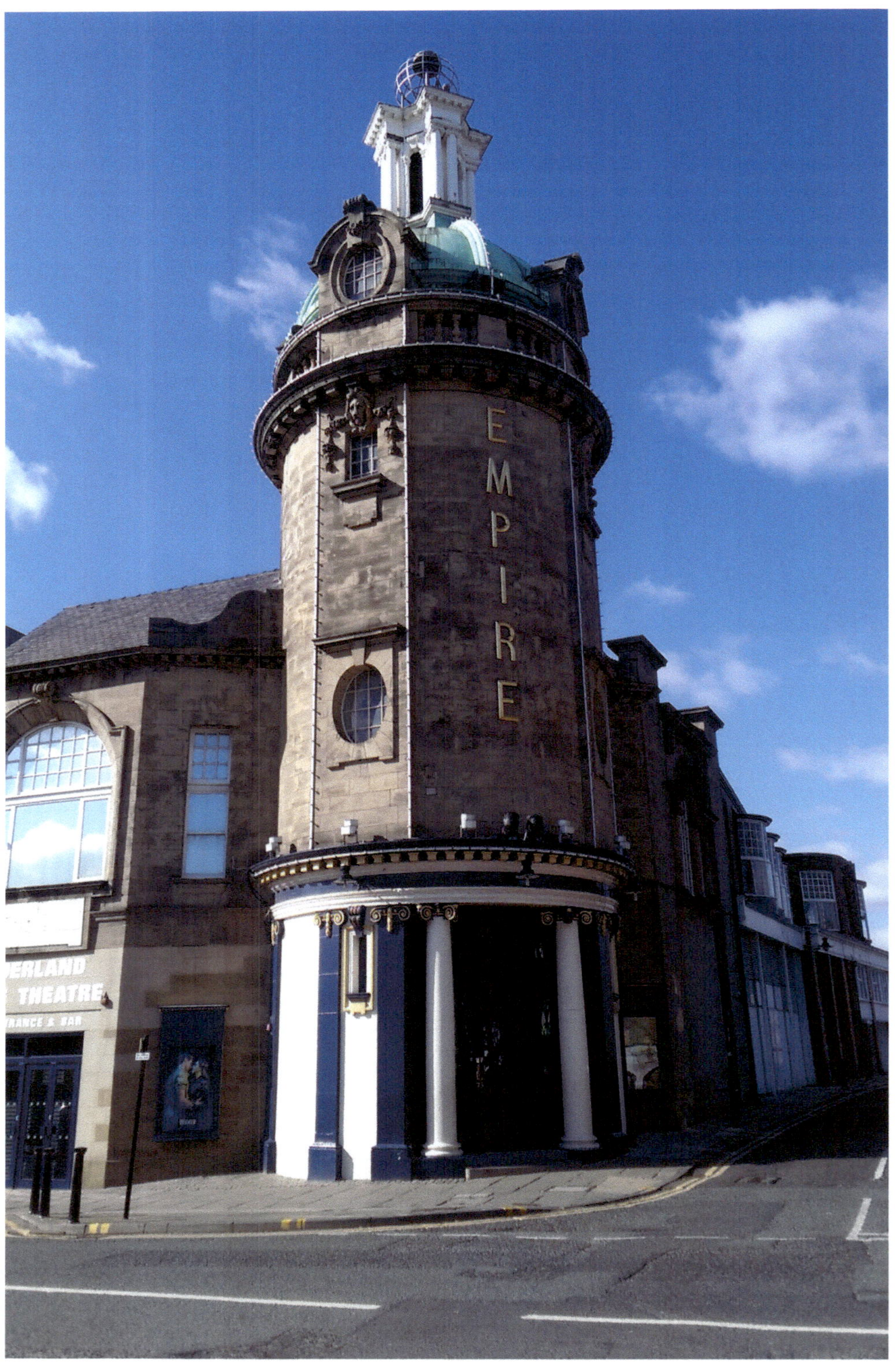

The Empire Theatre, Sunderland. (Used with the kind permission of Peter Woolford)

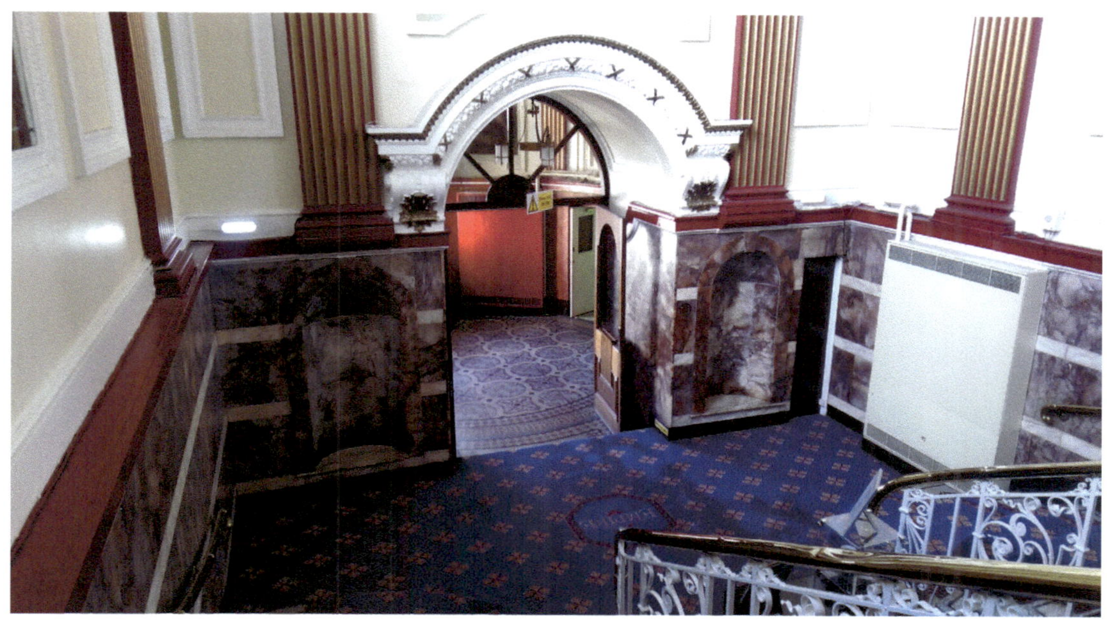

Above: The foyer. (Used with the kind permission of Peter Woolford)

Right: The auditorium. (Used with the kind permission of Peter Woolford)

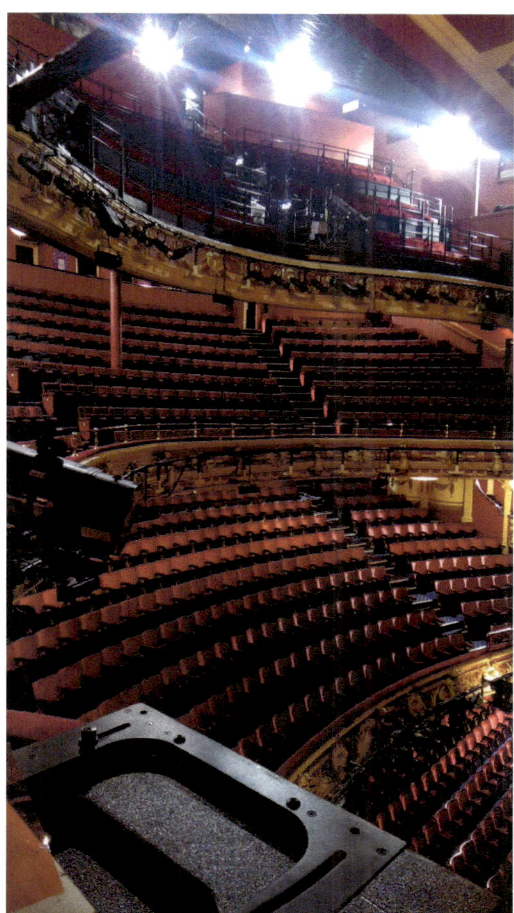

It is said she is watching from this area to make sure the theatre is safe and the performances go well. However, the sighting of this lady coincides with people reporting feeling uneasy in their seats and cold chills in the areas that she stands.

The third ghost story I have been told involves the local mystery of a young lady who disappeared in Sunderland. It is said that she returns to the Empire and interacts with guests in the bar area, and she is known to visit both men's and women's toilets. The spirit is believed to be that of Molly Burslem, or Molly Moselle as she was known on stage. She had been performing at the Empire throughout the winter months of 1949 and one day she suddenly vanished. The last time she was seen was when she left her home to post a letter near to the theatre and was never to return. A police investigation took place, but they never found any trace of her.

The people close to her had told the police that she had been involved with a couple of married men. However, both men had ended their relationships. Any thoughts of suicide were ruled out as they said she had such a happy and outgoing personality. We will possibly never find out what happened to Miss Molly unless someone can ask her if it is her visiting the theatre.

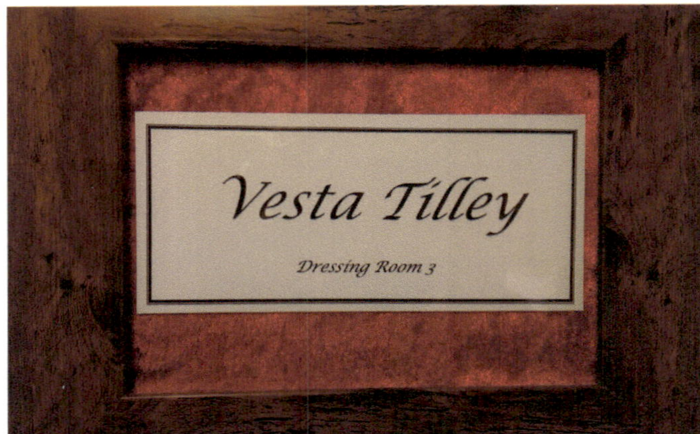

Left: Dressing Room of Vesta Tilley, whose ghost is said to still roam around the theatre. (Used with the kind permission of Peter Woolford)

Below: One of the many theatrical decorations. (Used with the kind permission of Peter Woolford)

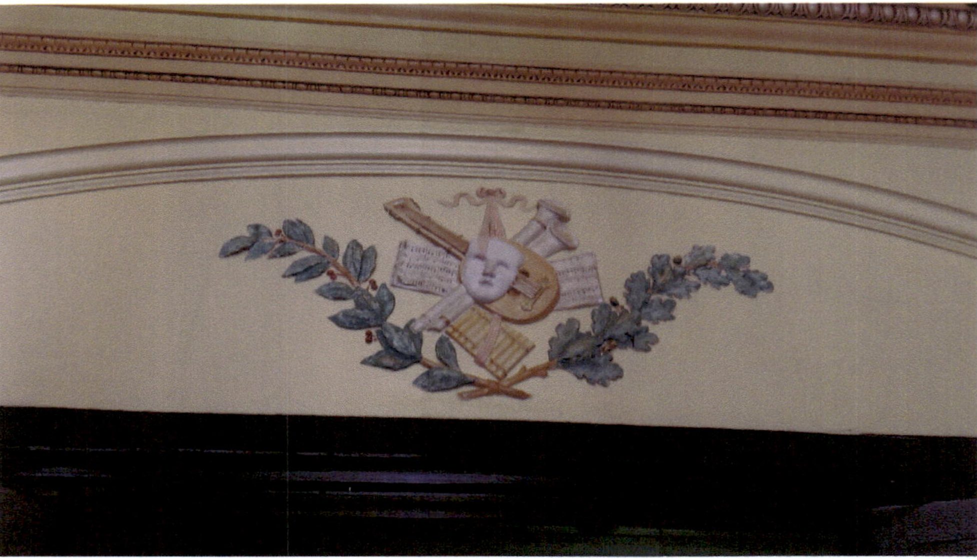

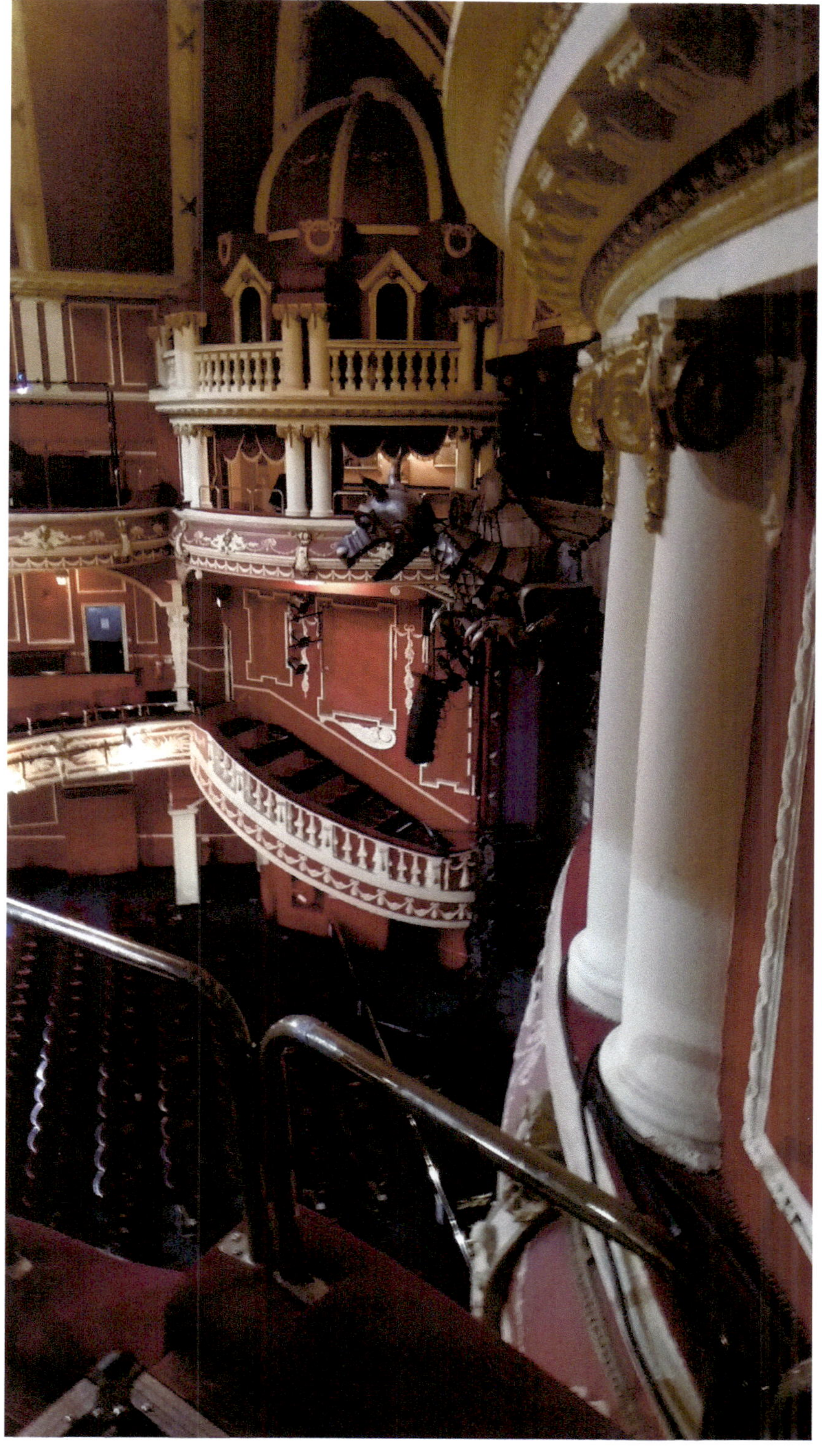

Looking down at the stage. (Used with the kind permission of Peter Woolford)

CHAPTER 10

The Holy Trinity Church

The east end of Sunderland on the southern bank of the Wear is the site of some of the oldest buildings that still stand in the city. At the top of the banks of the river and next to the Town Moor you will find a beautiful church. The Holy Trinity Church, or the 'Parish Church' as it is sometimes referred to, was built in 1719 due to the growth of the city. The other nearby church in Bishopwearmouth was getting oversubscribed and the local people started a campaign to get a new church constructed. The site was decided upon and an Act of Parliament was passed to create the new parish of Sunderland.

For 269 years the church bells rang out for services, weddings and funerals. However, unfortunately the church was to close in June 1988 due to a lack of worshippers. The church has remained closed for the past thirty years, but thankfully it is now undergoing a transformation and it will open as a community hall, serving the local community once again.

I have heard two different ghost stories about the Holy Trinity Church, but both involve its graveyard not the actual church. The first story involves the ghastly trade of grave robbing. Probably the most famous bodysnatchers were two Irish men called Burke and Hare, who would make a fortune during the 1820s robbing graves before deciding that murdering people was a quicker and easier way to produce dead bodies to sell to the local doctors. Burke and Hare were to visit Sunderland and work down on the local docks, although some reports say they were street traders selling food – I wouldn't like to imagine what food they would be peddling to the Sunderland public.

It's thought they quickly left Sunderland in 1824 and moved north to Edinburgh. In 1828, their crimes were uncovered in the Scottish capital, and they faced a trial for murder. Although the police knew of their grave-robbing activities, this was not deemed a crime at the time as corpses were not recognised as property. In January 1929, William Burke was found guilty and hanged in Edinburgh for his crimes. William Hare was never prosecuted as he turned his back on his friend and turned king's evidence for a deal of immunity.

During the 1820s and 1830s the Old Trinity Church was a victim of many grave robbing's. As it had the largest graveyard in the area, which led directly on to the Town Moor, it gave the bodysnatchers an easy getaway. On moonless nights or when the thick North Sea fog rolled in, it gave the ideal opportunity to snatch and run without being seen; however, their lights are still seen to this day. There have been many sightings of lights in the graveyard on dark nights or when the mist rolls in. When people shout or go into the graveyard to see what is going on, the lights flee across the graves and out onto the Town Moor to simply disappear.

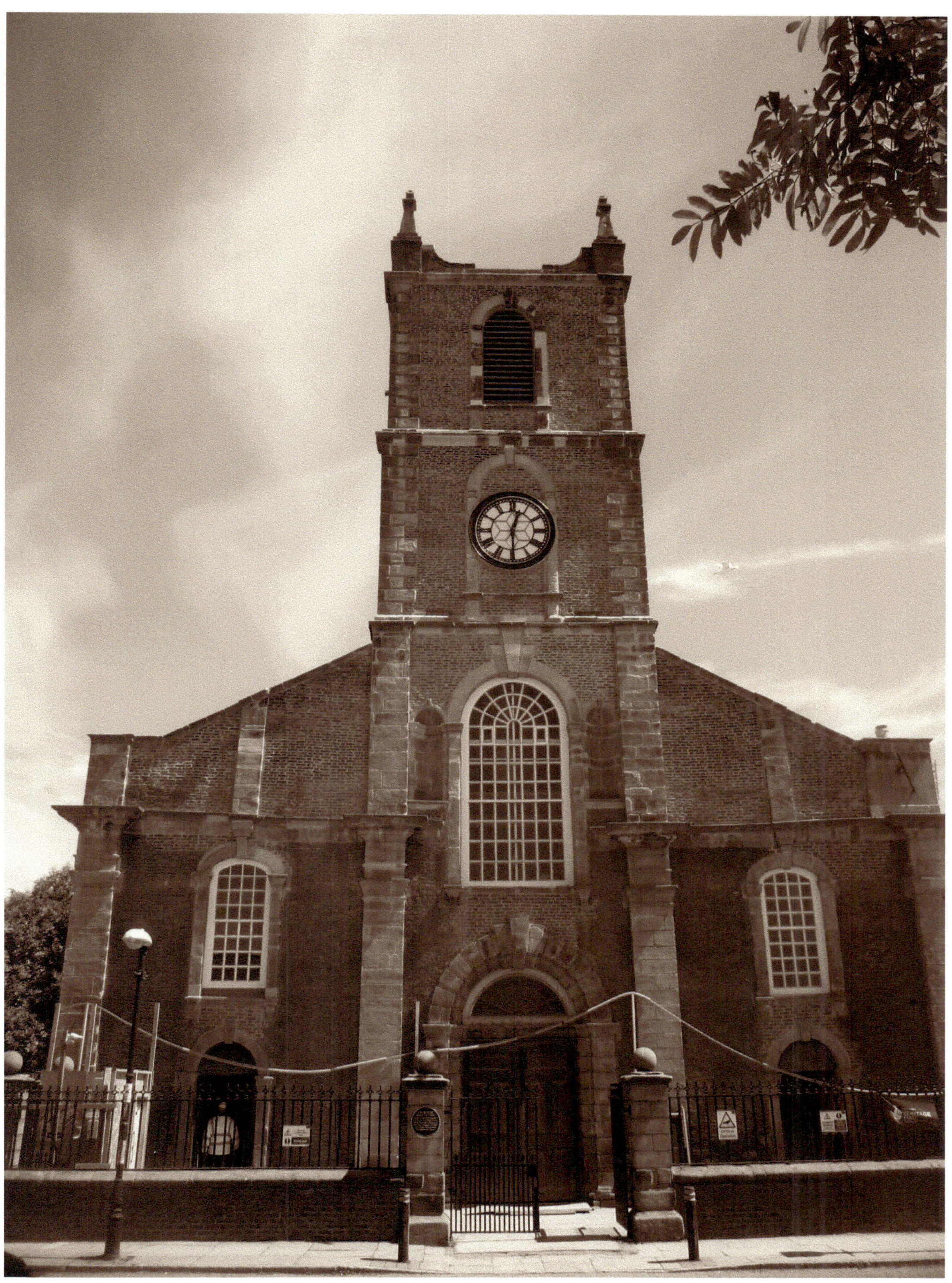

The entrance to the church.

One eyewitness said he was walking past, coming from the Town Moor onto Church Street East, when he saw two men in the graveyard. He said it was a dark and foggy night and he was straining to see what they were up to, so he walked into the graveyard to get closer. He described two men dressed in Victorian clothing; one carrying what looked like a shovel and one with an old-fashioned lamp. As he got closer, he shouted at them and asked what they were doing. The men turned and looked at him, started to laugh and ran through the fence, then disappeared into the fog on the moor. The man said he was shaking for days as he clearly saw the men run straight through the fence – not over it.

Who did he see on that night? Could it have been the infamous Mr Burke and Mr Hare, or was it the ghosts of another pair of unscrupulous rapscallions still plying their trade in the afterlife?

The second story from the graveyard involves the sighting of a young sailor saluting. He appears next to one of the memorials and is often seen on or around 11 October, which makes us think it is the ghost of Jack Crawford.

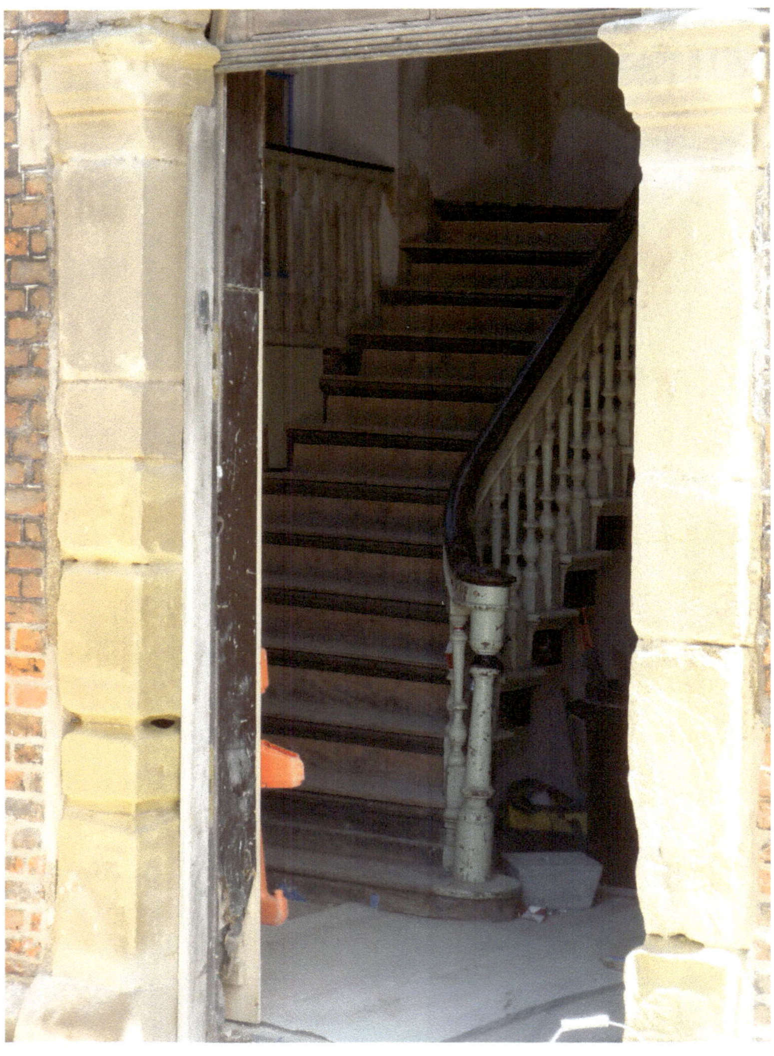

Stairway leading to the upper floor.

Jack was a local lad from Sunderland's east end who worked on the local boats. In 1786, he joined the Royal Navy and became a member of the crew of HMS *Venerable*. As the French Revolutionary War raged, the Dutch Navy launched an attack on the British and the HMS *Venerable* became the flagship during the Battle of Camperdown.

At the start of the battle on 11 October 1797, a Dutch cannonball ripped through the mast of the *Venerable*, causing it to collapse bringing down the Admiral's flag. The lowering of the Admiral flag was a sign of surrender and would have been a catastrophe for the fleet. Quick-thinking Jack decided to climb up the mast and nailed the flag back above the ship – hence the well-known saying 'nail your colours to the mast'. The battle continued and the British Navy recorded a famous victory by defeating the Dutch without losing any of their fleet.

Jack was welcomed back to England with a hero's reception, complete with a medal and a meeting with the king, before moving back to Sunderland. Unfortunately, Jack fell afoul of his own hype and ended up battling the demon drink before dying a pauper in 1831 from cholera.

So, if you are passing his memorial at the Holy Trinity Church around 11 October and you see the young sailor, be sure to salute the famous Jack Crawford.

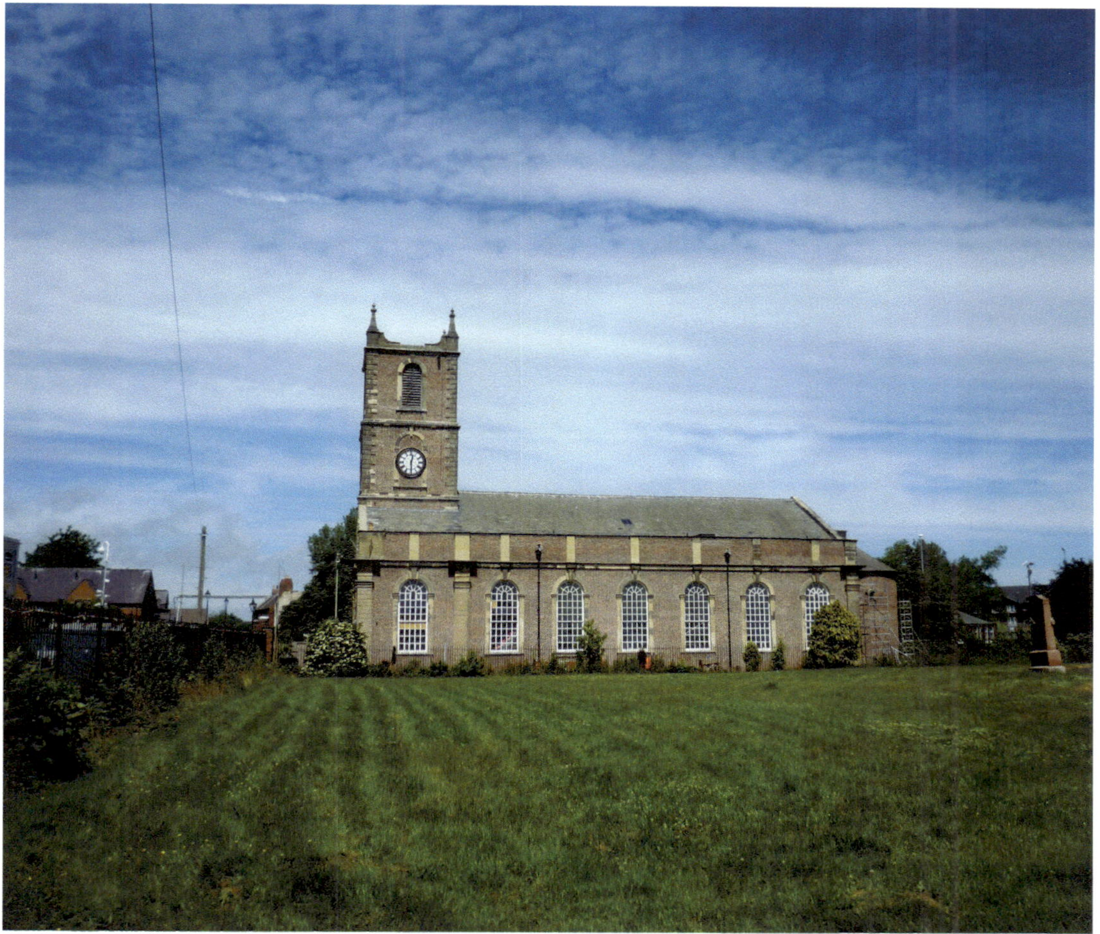

The church and the large graveyard.

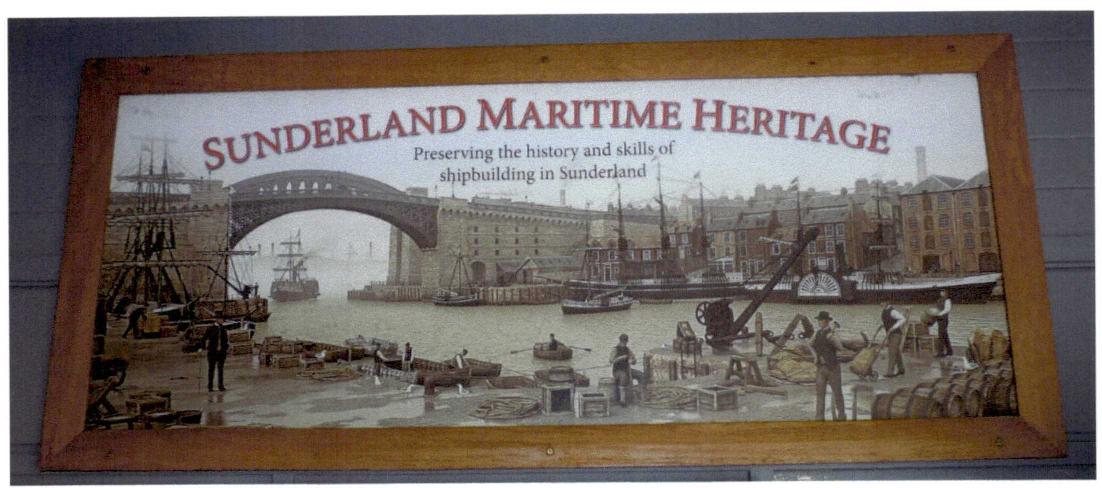

Sunderland Maritime Heritage Museum.

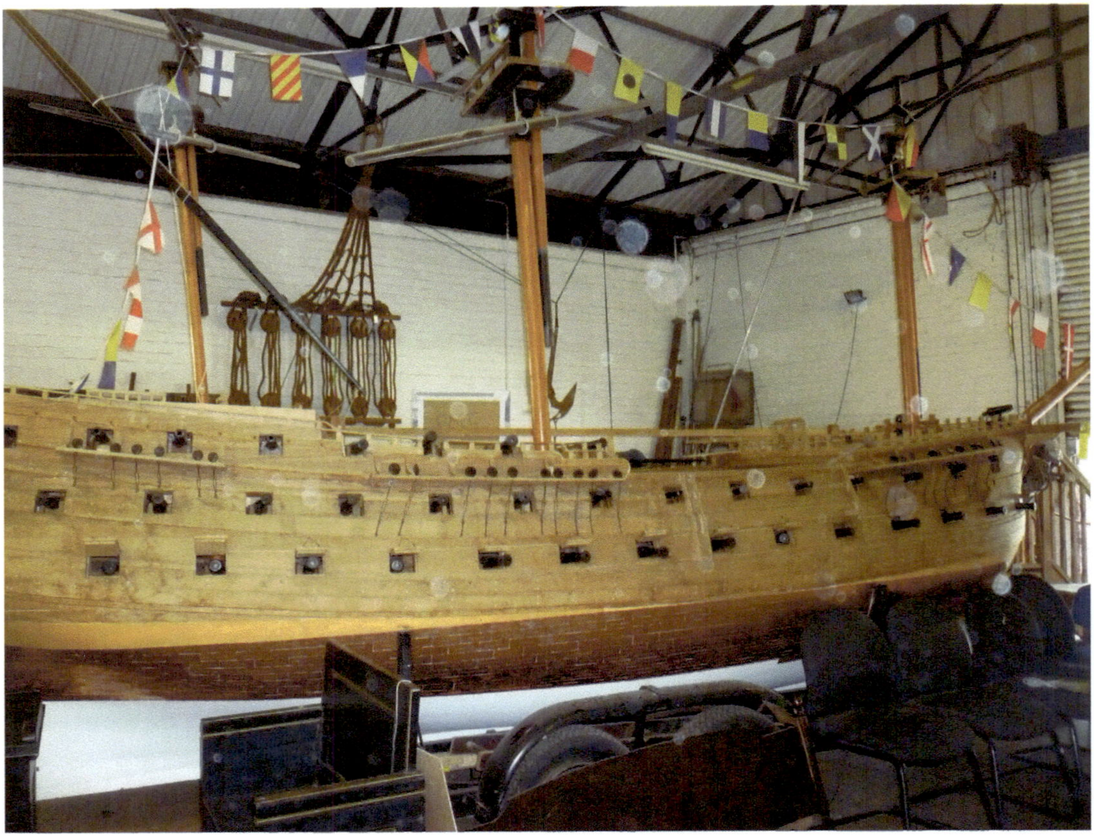

A model of HMS *Venerable*, the ship on which Jack Crawford served.

CHAPTER 11

The Blue Girl of Low Street

Over the years I have heard this ghost story many times and what is interesting is that it never occurs in the same place. Granted, it is always on Low Street, but I've been told it was spotted near the lobster pots of the Fish Quay, near to the entrance of the docks and also as far west as the fantastic mural celebrating S. F. Austin & Sons Shipbuilding that Frank Styles painted for the visit of the Tall Ships.

But before I tell you the story of 'the Blue Girl', we have to travel back in time to 1831 when Sunderland was an extremely busy port and hundreds of boats would come and go from the river transporting coal, glass and pottery from the surrounding area to customers around the world. Elsewhere in the world there was an outbreak of cholera that was spreading east from India and had recently run rife through Russia and across Europe. It had been renamed 'Cholera Morbus', as it killed fast and was different to the cholera that England had seen before.

With this in mind, the authorities ordered all ships from Russia or any Baltic ports to be quarantined before being allowed to dock on the British mainland. However, the port of Sunderland didn't agree and ignored the privy council, and in October 1831 Sunderland became the first place in Britain to report an outbreak of Cholera Morbus.

It was reported that the first case of the disease was a local keelman called William Sproat, who died after three days of sickness on 26 October. However, this was not true as a young twelve-year-old girl called Isabella Hazard had died a week prior to this on Low Street and had displayed all the symptoms of the Cholera Morbus, including the most striking symptom of the skin taking a blue hue due to dehydration.

It took them nearly two weeks to inform the authorities of the cholera outbreak and by then it was spreading across the country fast, taking over 200 souls in Sunderland before dying out by the start of 1832. The nationwide outbreak would claim more than 50,000 souls.

The ghost story around Low Street is that people have seen a young girl either sitting or lying on the floor crying. She has a shawl wrapped around her head and shoulders. The witnesses have walked up to her and, when they get close, they are startled as her face is blue. Many have turned and run for help only for the girl to have vanished on their return. One witness said she spoke to the girl and asked her name and she replied, 'Isabella'. The witness stood up and rang 999 on her mobile phone. As the emergency services connected she looked back down to the girl, but she had gone. The witness then had to apologise and say she had made a mistake, but still swears to this day she met Isabella Hazard, 'the Blue Girl' of Low Street.

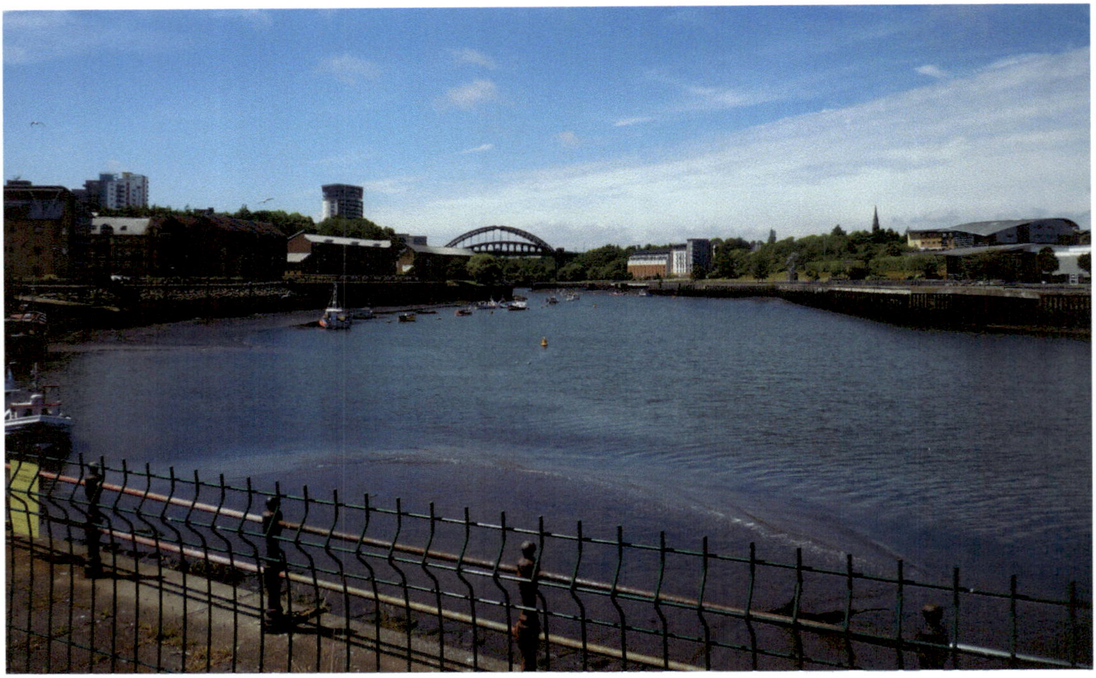

Paranormal Sunderland

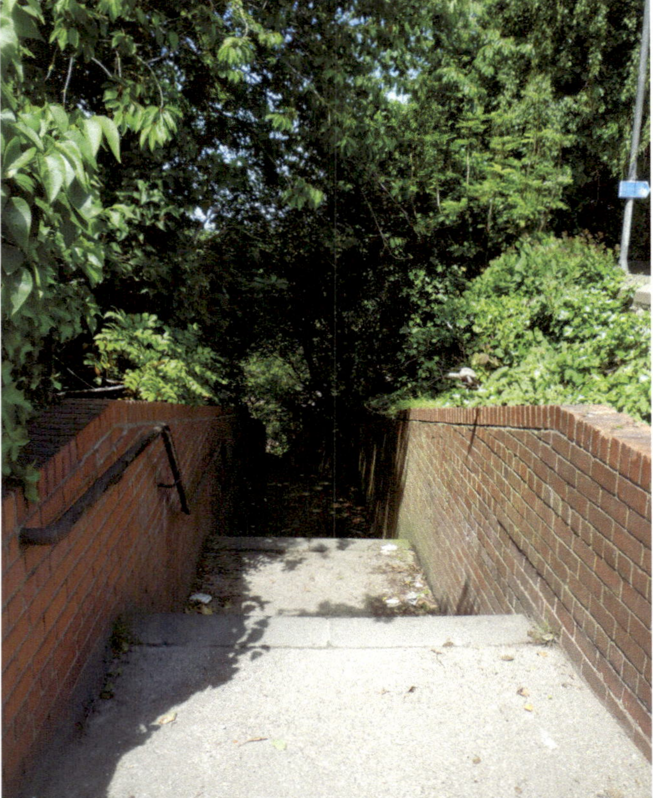

Above: Sunderland Quayside.

Left: Footpath down to the Quay, where the Blue Girl has been spotted.

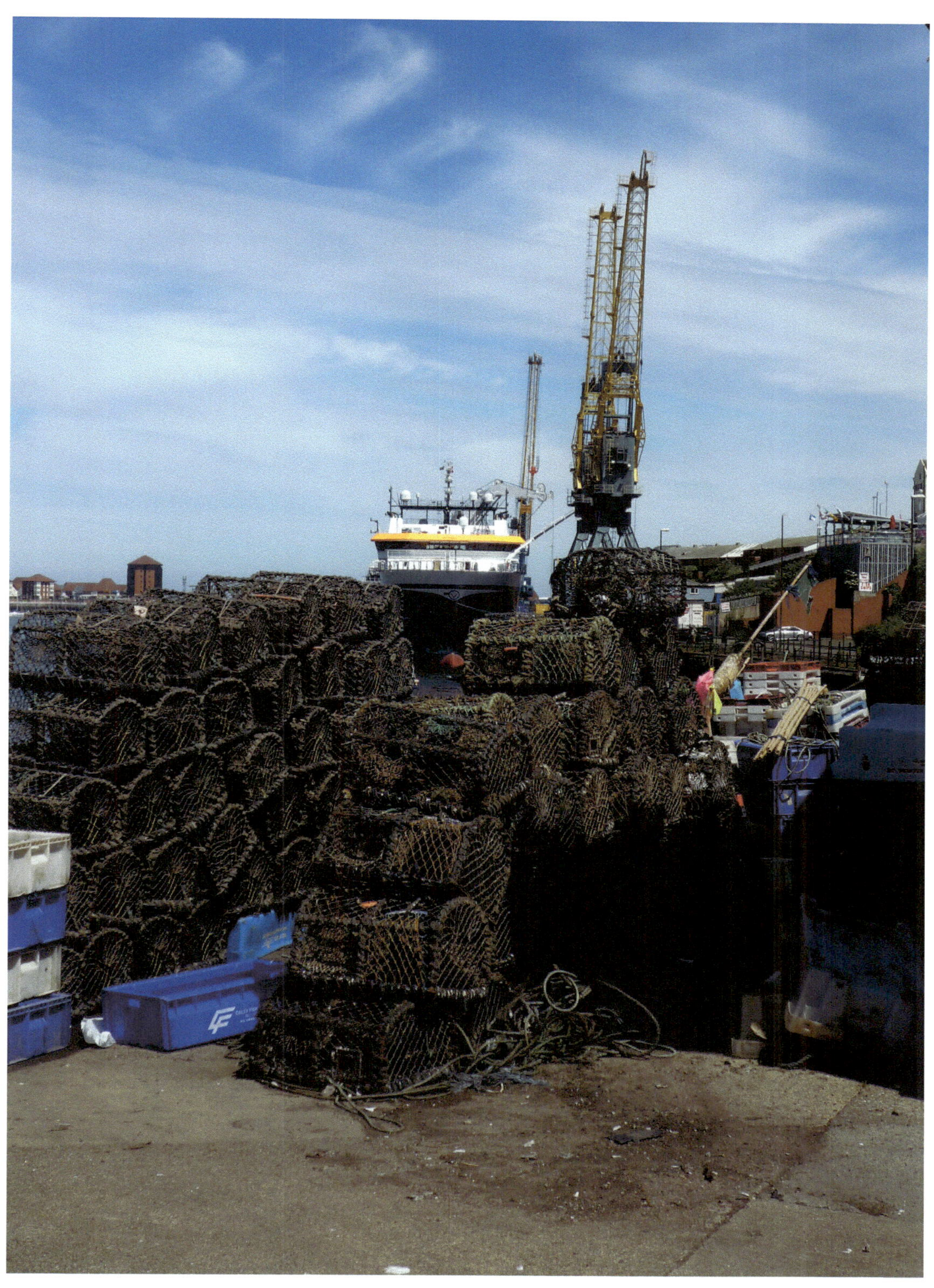

Lobster pots near to Sunderland Docks.

CHAPTER 12

Panns Bank

Staying on the quayside, there is an area called Panns Bank. The area is named after the Wearmouth Salt Panns and dates back to at least the sixteenth century. The salt pan industry was common throughout Britain, and Sunderland was no different, as it used the salty sea water in the mouth of the river.

Small swallow ponds of sea water were made and then left for several days for the water to evaporate naturally. This left a layer of salt on top of the mud. This watery mix would be sent to a boiling house and the water boiled away, leaving the natural sea salt, which would be sold across the world.

This area of Sunderland is also historic due to the English Civil War. In 1644, the area was better known as the Bishopwearmouth Panns and was a settlement for the Scottish Army for three years, as they joined forces with the Parliamentarians to rage war against the Royalists and Charles I.

Sunderland had already shown an allegiance with Oliver Cromwell and his Parliamentarians as London had throttled Sunderland's coal trade thirty years earlier by enforcing a tax payable to Newcastle. Newcastle had always been supporters of the king and the Scottish wanted to use their base in Sunderland to attack Newcastle from the south. This encampment would see battles in Hylton, Boldon and South Shields, before finally marching across the Tyne.

An old friend told me a story about Panns Bank and I'm going to tell it just as he told me. I will say he was neither a believer nor sceptic of the paranormal as he had never really taken a great deal of notice of the subject, so I was surprised when he said he had to tell someone what had happened.

In an untraditional start to a ghost story, it all happened on a sunny day in June. He was walking along the quayside and was planning to walk along the riverside to the far side of the bridge with his dog. He was not a native of Sunderland, having moved to the area when he found employment at the Nissan car plant; therefore, he knew little of the history of the area, and again it was not something he was really interested in.

As he walked past Panns Bank, his dog started to act very peculiarly. His Labrador, who he had owned for many years, started to run back to him and seemed to not want to walk further up the path without him. This, he said, was strange as she usually would run in front until he whistled. As he walked further on, confused by the dog's hesitation, the dog suddenly stopped still and stared at the river. The tide was out, and down on the riverside was a small group of men wearing old clothing and blue cloth caps. Next to them was a Scottish flag on the end of a small stick.

At the time my friend said although I did think it must be dangerous down there, I thought it must be some sort of military re-enactment or one of these historic groups as they didn't look bothered by their surroundings. My friend called out with a simple 'hello', but no one replied. 'Actually, they didn't even look up', he said. He thought he would take a couple of pictures on his phone to show his wife when he got home. He then carried on walking before turning back some time later. He said that as he returned to his car the tide had come in and the men were gone, and he didn't give it a thought until he got home.

He started to recall the story to his wife and expressed that they were a bit rude as they didn't even look up when he spoke to them. However, it was when he produced his phone to show her the photographs that he received the biggest shock as there was no one on them. The photos were just shots of the riverbank. His wife laughed and said he needed to improve his photography skills, but my friend insisted the men should be in the pictures and even pointed out where they had been standing.

After several days of telling people the story and showing them the photographs, some the locals explained the history of the Panns and the army camp during the Civil War. When he came to me and recounted the tale, he was convinced he had seen the ghosts of the Scottish soldiers of past wars. Unfortunately, my friend is no longer with us as he was taken too soon. However, I'm sure he would have been honoured to know that I have shared his story in this book. Rest in peace, Mr C.

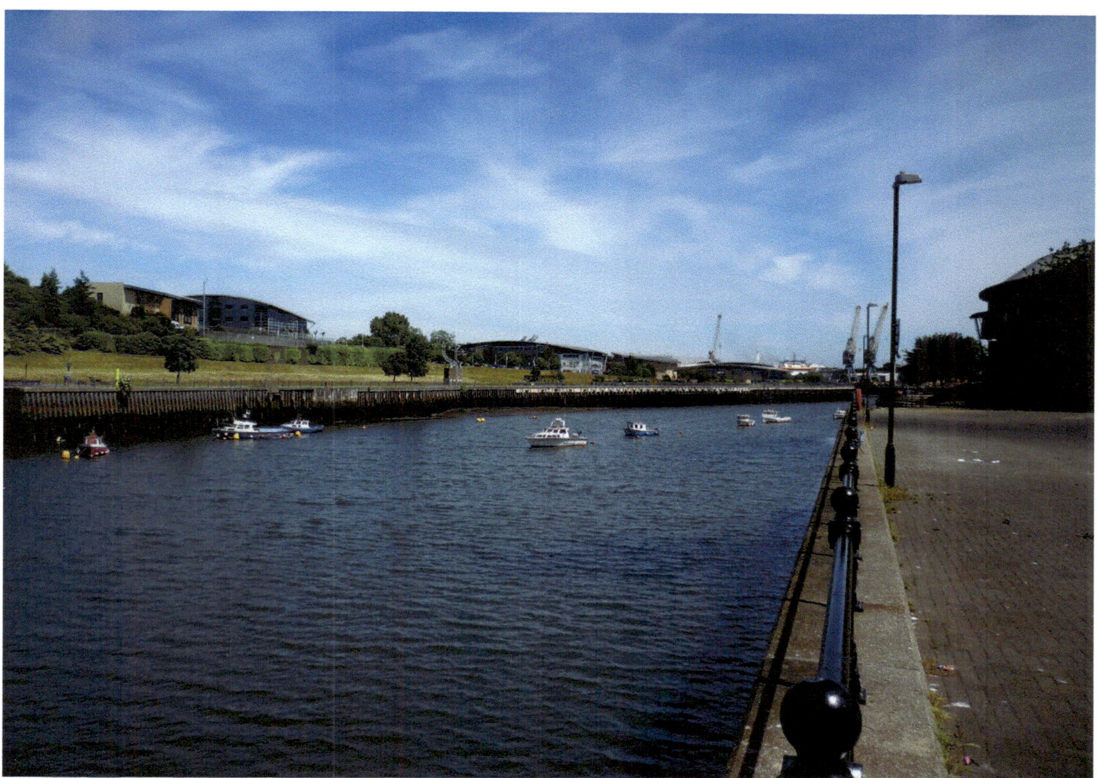

The River Wear.

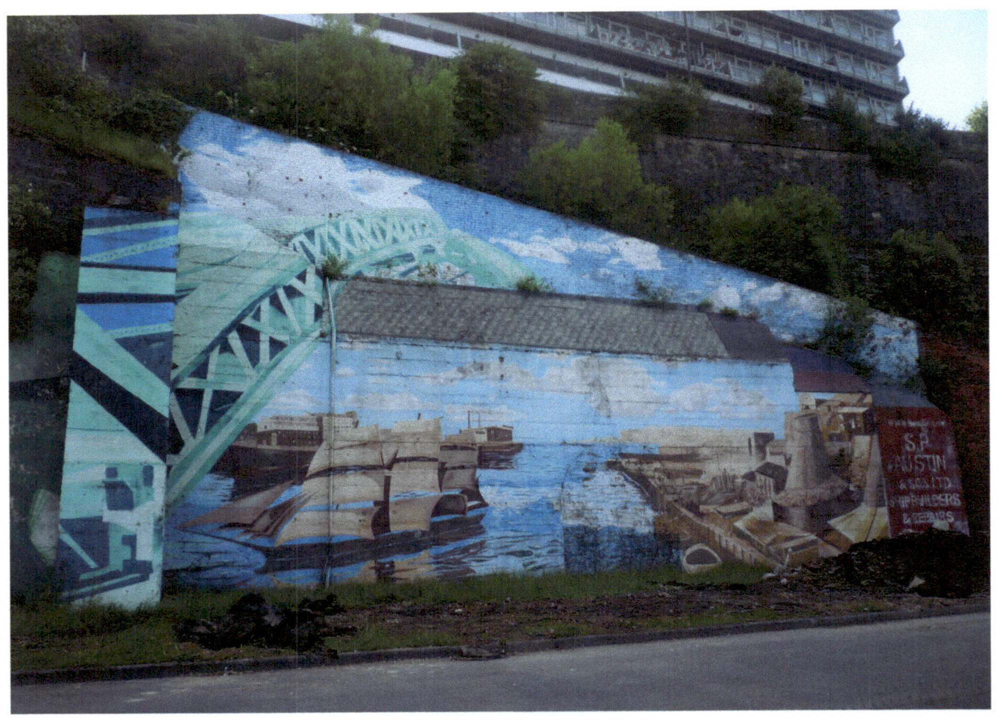

Above: Mural celebrating shipbuilding in the city.

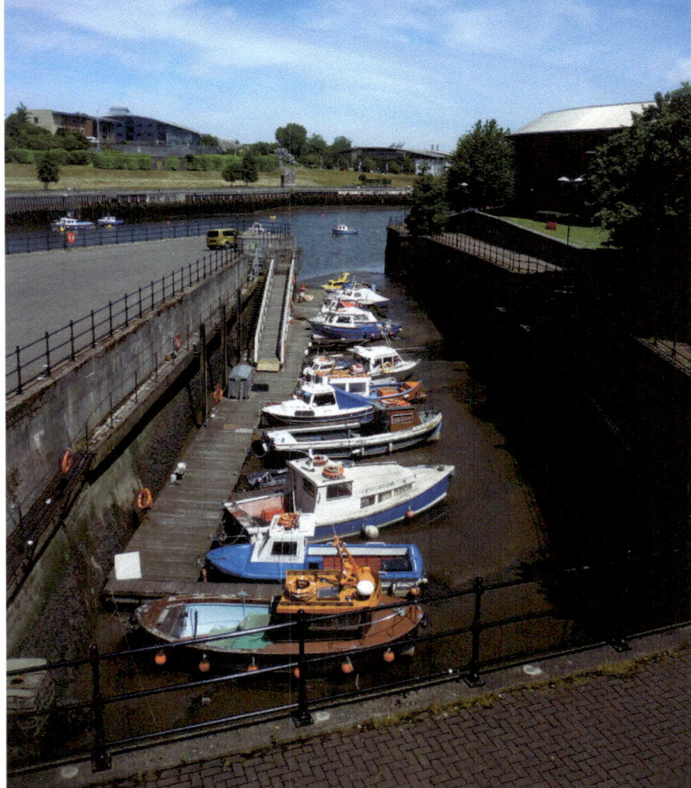

Left: Boats near Panns Bank.

CHAPTER 13

The Shipwrights Arms

As you travel down the bank to the riverside in North Hylton, you will see the sign for the Shipwrights Arms that proudly informs you that it is the oldest pub in Sunderland, and as you turn onto the lane and see the pub you feel like you have been transported back 350 years into the past.

Although the building has been updated for a more modern customer, from the outside it has all the charm and beauty of an eighteenth-century coaching inn. As you stand outside on the riverbanks it is easy to imagine the area bustling during the 1700s – it stands near to the ferry point that would take traffic across the Wear as it travelled between Newcastle and Durham. Opposite, you can still see where ships have been built and launched from the southern banks. However, on darker days when the weather is being typically northern, or on a cold winter evening, it is easier to imagine the more sinister activities that were taking place, including smuggling and press ganging.

Press ganging was rife throughout the seventeenth and eighteenth centuries and, surprisingly, was authorised by Parliament to help the Royal Navy fulfil their conscription during the many wars and naval battles that were raging off the coasts of Europe.

Sunderland was no different from any other town in the country, and Ferryboat Lane, with its coaching inns, was a popular place for the press gangers to nab highly intoxicated young men and throw them straight onto the boats docked on the riverside. This would include a quick whack to the back of the head with a small wooden club, a bag over the head and a quick wrestle onto the boat, or at times a full-on fight, which never ended well for the drunken locals.

There are many reports of men shouting in the area late at night along Ferryboat Lane and when people look to see who is making all the noise, no one is to be seen in the area. Dark figures have been seen running along the riverbank before strangely disappearing over the edge into the river.

A story that has been told for many years is about a young man being chased into the Shipwrights Arms by a small group of uniformed men, only for the men never to appear inside the pub – at times the door to the pub was even closed and locked. Have these people seen a press gang giving chase to an unfortunate local from times gone by?

Another story is that of a woman who is seen wandering the corridor upstairs before walking through the doors into several of the coaching inn's rooms. The reports come from both staff and guests. They all describe her as a pretty lady and wearing very smart Victorian or earlier style of dress. Unlike most ghost stories, she is said to be smiling and people don't feel afraid as she floats between rooms. Nothing is known of the woman, whether she is one of the past landladies, staff members or maybe one of the many ladies of the night that earned a crust from the numerous visitors to the coaching inn in days gone by.

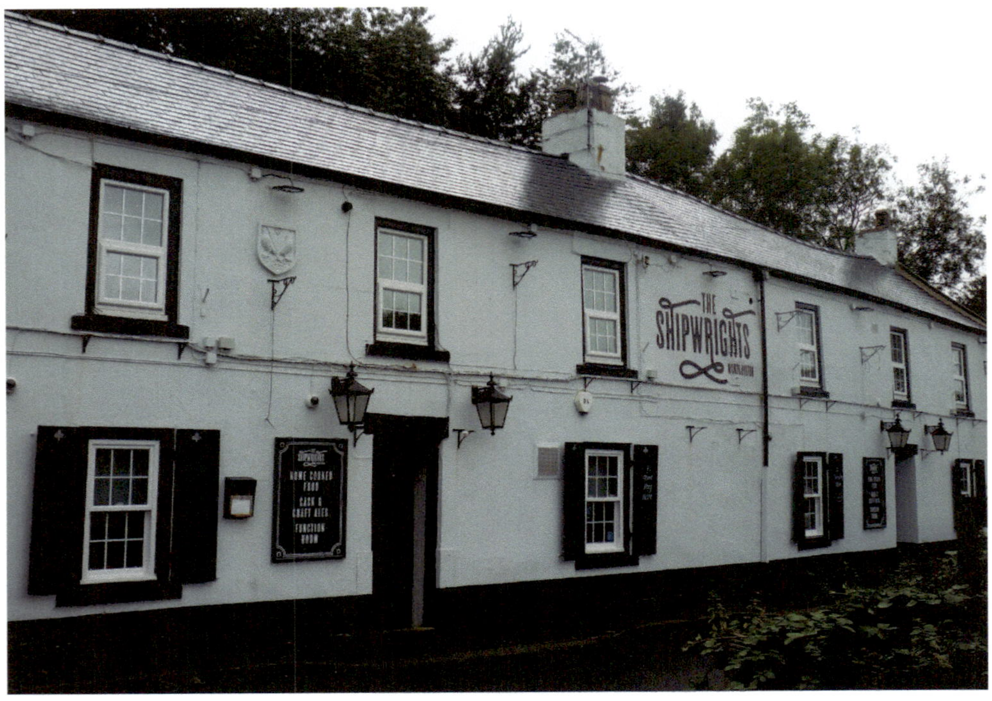

An original coaching inn.

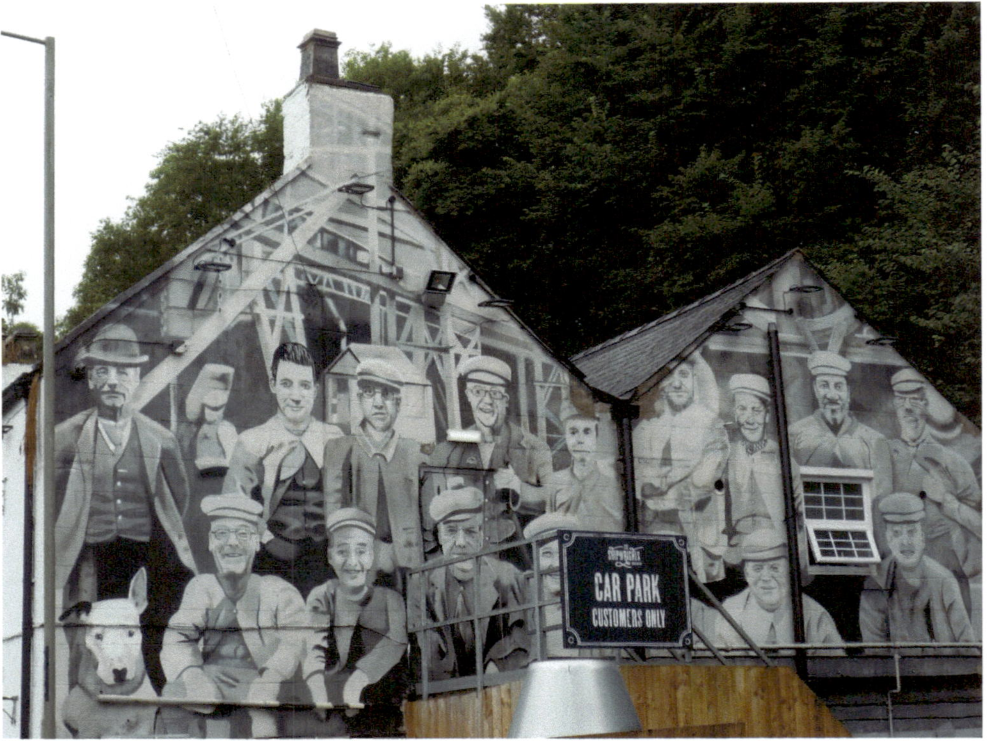

A mural on the side of the pub as a tribute to the local men.

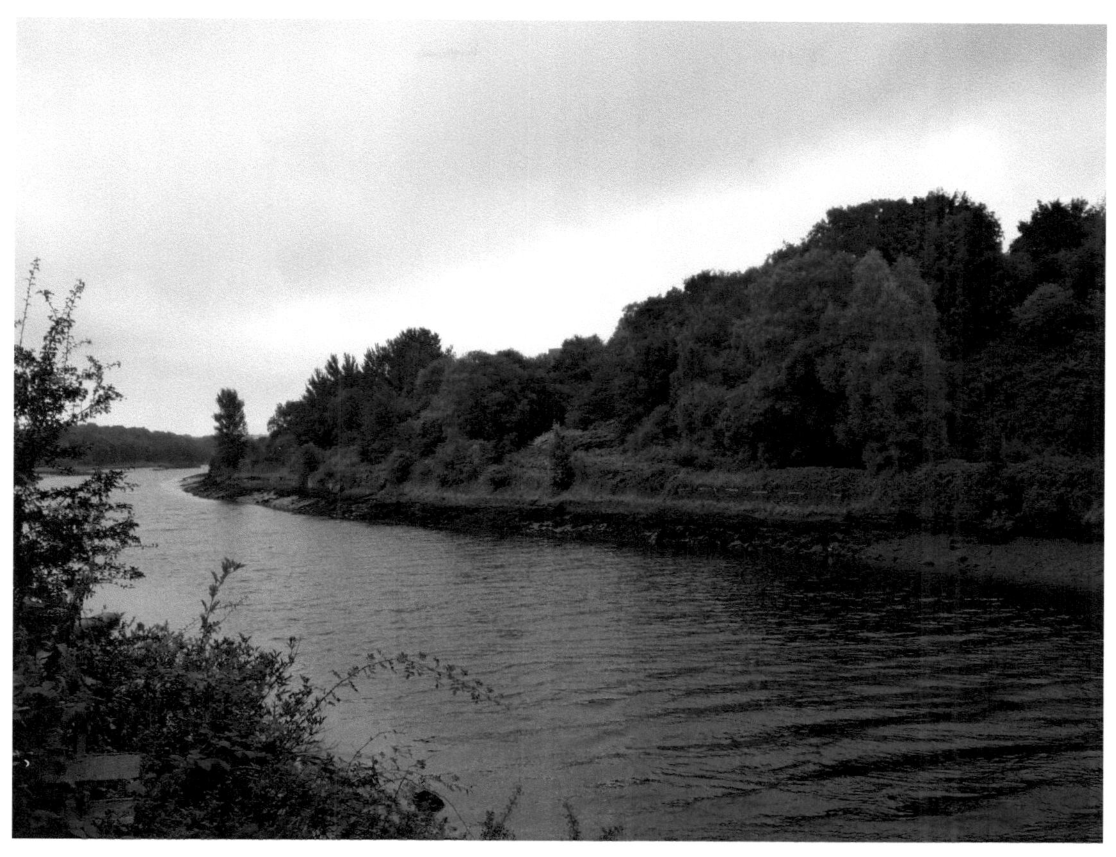

The riverside that led to many men being press-ganged.

CHAPTER 14

The Stadium of Light

The Stadium of Light is located on the northern banks of the river, near to the bridges that link the two parts of the city and is home to Sunderland Association Football Club. As I mentioned in the introduction, I am a lifelong Sunderland supporter and I have seen my fair share of ghost defences and disappearing players down on the pitch over the years. Joking aside, the stadium is said to be one of the most haunted stadiums in the world.

The stadium was only opened in July 1997 as the new home of the football club after they had to leave the nearby Roker Park. So, the building is relatively new, but it still has its fair share of ghost stories.

Sometimes when I'm asked why a new building would be haunted, I will often say that it is worth investigating the land on which it stands. The Stadium of Light is a location that fits that description. The stadium was built on top of Monkwearmouth Colliery. The colliery was opened in 1835 and was to become the largest in Sunderland, boasting the deepest mine shaft in the world at 1,720 feet at the time of opening.

The colliery became imperative to Sunderland during the twentieth century as it employed over 2,000 people above and below the ground. It became the last mine to operate in the County Durham Coalfield before it finally closed in December 1993.

During the 158 years of operating as a colliery, over 200 miners sadly lost their lives during their shifts, including two major tragedies. The first was in September 1862 when a shaft collapsed and killed five men. Then in May 1869 an explosion killed seven unfortunate souls. The colliery was cleared after the closure and five years later had been transformed into the stadium and its surrounding amenities.

But it is in the actual stadium that the ghosts are spotted, and these sightings have mostly been by staff. It was reported that dark figures have been seen walking through the upper-floor corridors in the supporter areas behind the seats, and figures have even been seen walking across the pitch only for them to disappear halfway.

The figures were spotted on Sky Sports' *Monday Night Football* show. During the broadcast of Sunderland's defeat to Everton in September 2016, a figure appears behind Jamie Carragher before disappearing into thin air and reappearing behind Phil Neville a few minutes later. A theory shared by Capital FM was that Adrian Partridge, who was the groundsman at the time, had been filmed earlier and was on a film loop that is played behind the panel. Although Sky Sports have never confirmed nor denied this, it does sound a reasonable explanation. Have a look on the internet as the footage is still there and decide for yourself.

I booked myself on a stadium tour a few years ago and I must admit that when you walk around on a Thursday afternoon and there are no supporters around, it does become a very eerie place. I asked the tour guide about the ghosts and she replied that they try not to talk about it anymore as it used to spook the players and some of the staff, but she could confirm that the figures were still seen.

These stories are not to be confused with stories from the training ground up the road at the Academy or the story of Spottee of Roker, both of which I will cover in further chapters of the book.

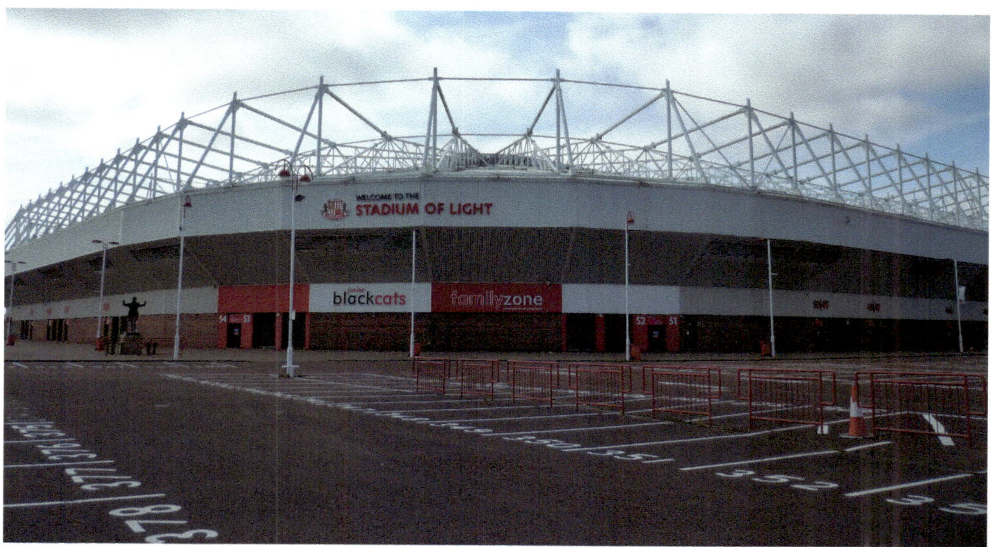

Outside of the stadium.

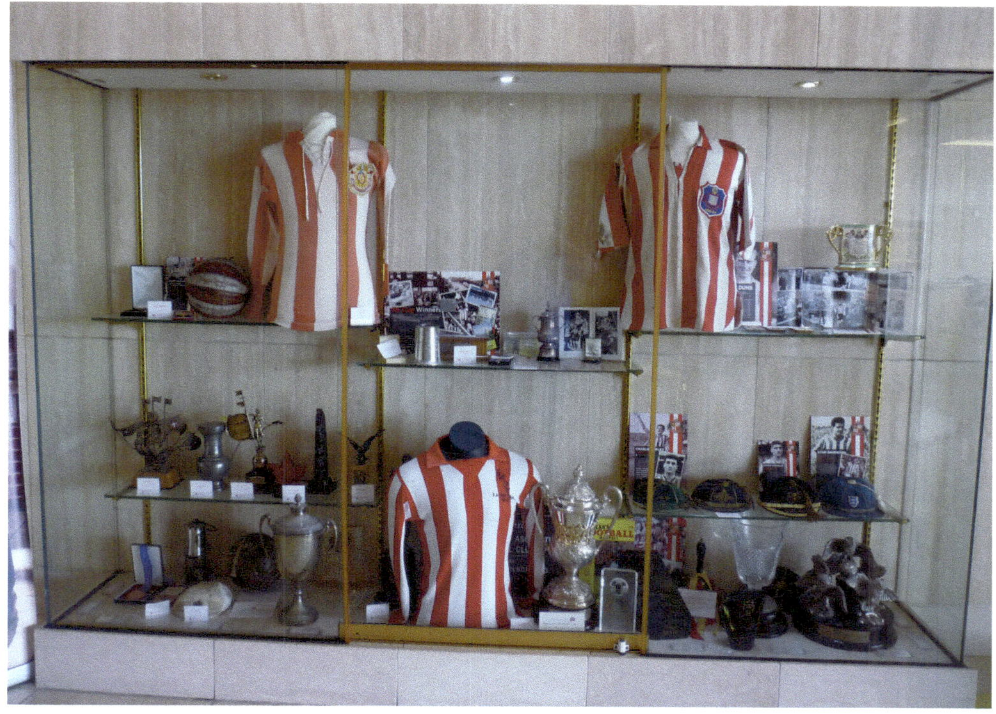

Inside the stadium corridors.

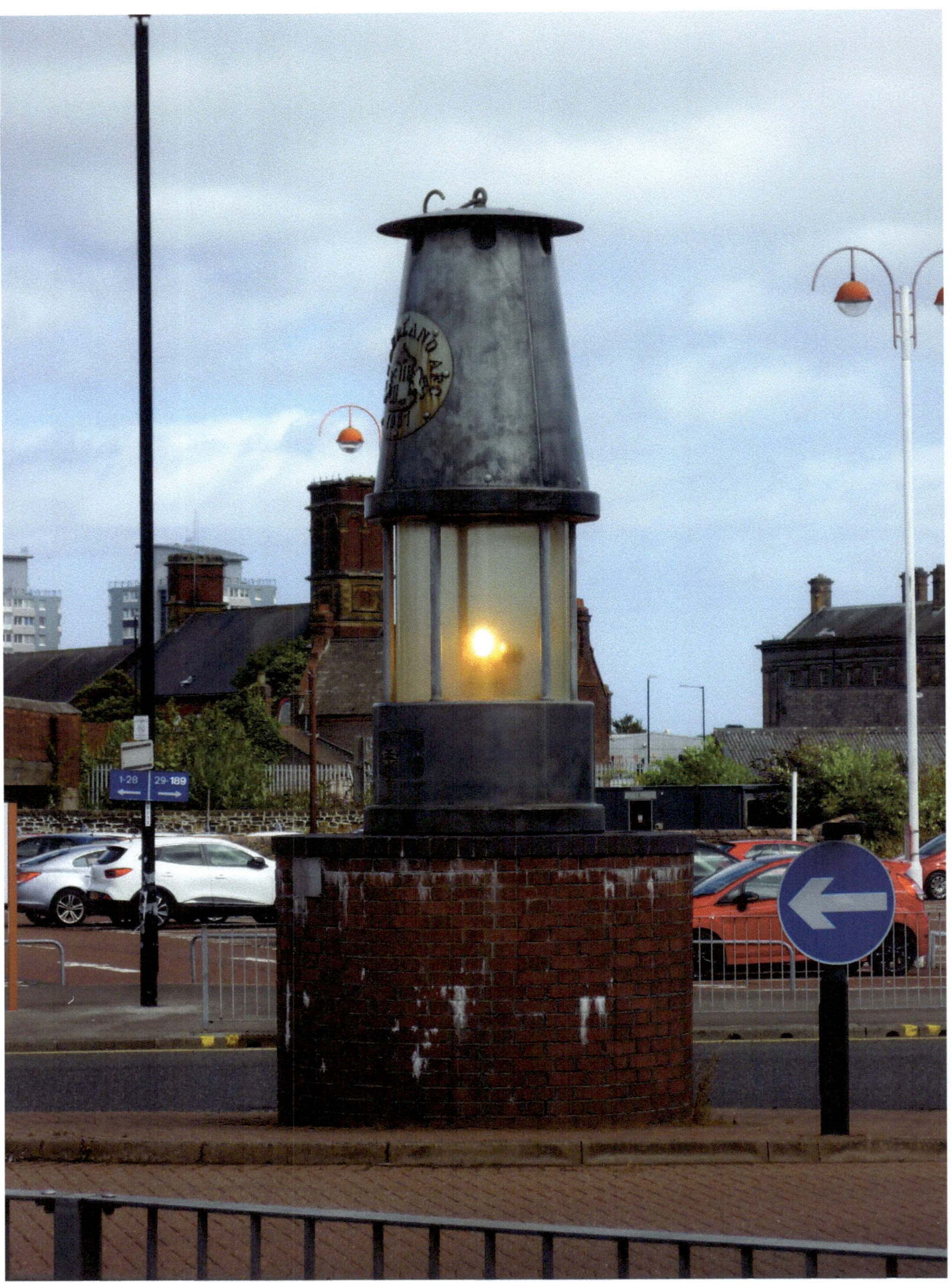

Memorial to the coal miners of Monkwearmouth.

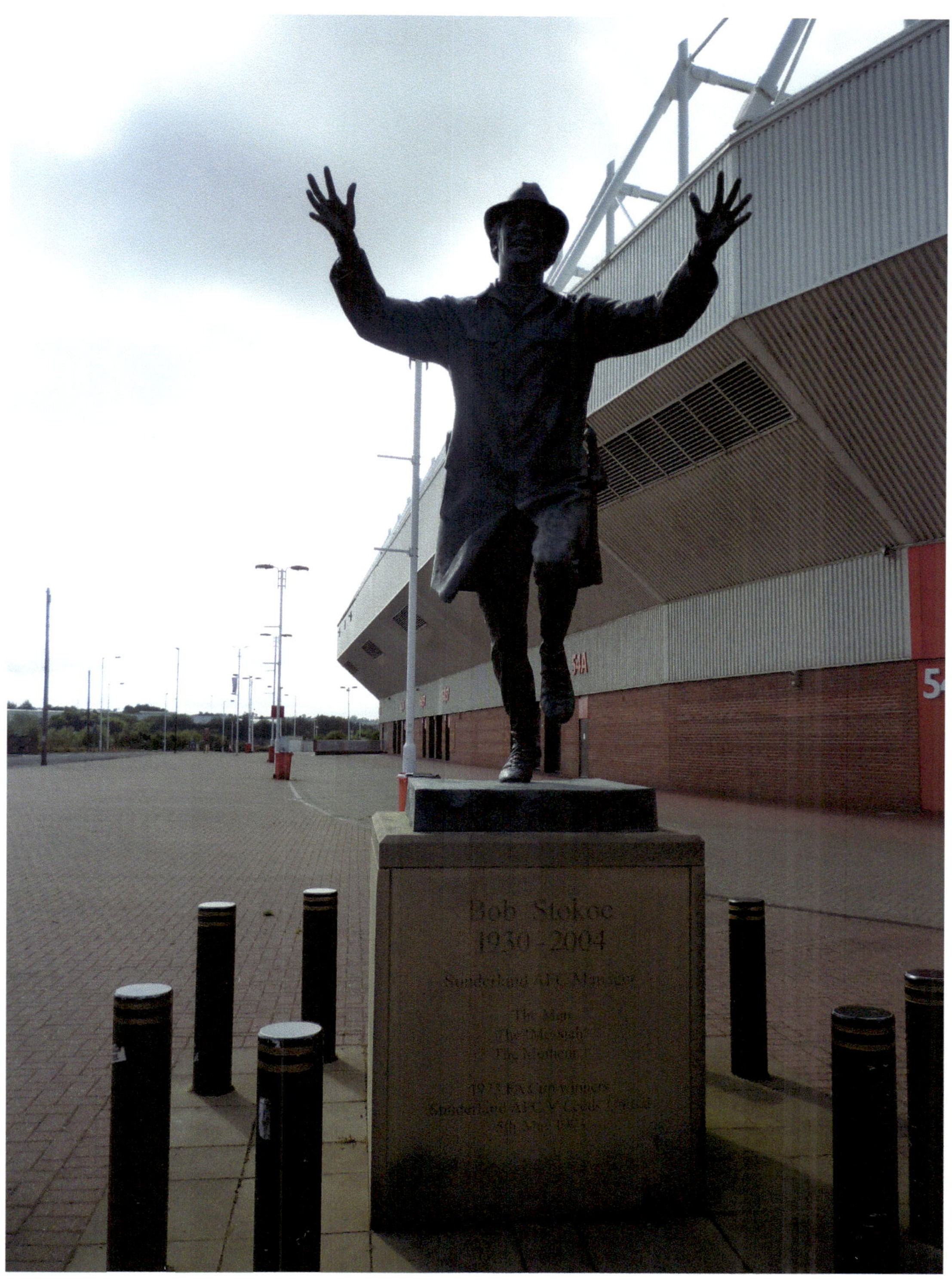

Statue of Bob Stokoe.

CHAPTER 15

The Ship Isis

Mary Ann Cotton, she's dead and she's rotten.
Lying in bed with her eyes wide open.
Sing, sing, oh what should I sing?
Mary Ann Cotton, she's tied up with string.
Where, where? Up in the air.
Selling black puddings, a penny a pair.

Above is a well-known children's nursery rhyme that tells the story of one of the most notorious residents of Sunderland. Mary Ann Cotton gained her infamy by becoming Britain's first female serial killer, murdering up to twenty-one people including three of her husbands and eleven of her children. It is believed she poisoned them over a number of years to claim the insurance. She was not caught until 1873.

When her trial took place and she was found guilty of the murder of one man: her then husband, Charles Cotton. She pleaded innocent all the way to the gallows as she was sentenced to death. She was hanged in Durham Gaol on 24 March 1873 and the enormity of her crimes became public knowledge.

When writing this book her name came up time and again and I was told numerous stories about the ghost of Mary Ann. Most of the stories were tales that people had been told as children in the same vein as the bogeyman, such as: 'If you don't behave Mary Ann Cotton will come and get you.'

As she had lived in various parts of Sunderland – such as Hendon, Pallion and Seaham Harbour – as well as County Durham, I delved deeper into the stories and was told to visit the Ship Isis. This is a pub located on Silksworth Row in the Millfield area of Sunderland and opened its doors in 1885. The Grade II listed Victorian building is a stunning reminder of the old architecture of Sunderland and is still operating as a public house to this day, serving pints to generations of Sunderland families for over 130 years. However, it is also well known for its paranormal activity and has been referred to as one of the most haunted pubs in Sunderland.

A young lady who was a bartender for some years told me that there were numerous reports of activity in the bar area, including glasses smashing, chairs and tables moving, and odd light anomalies and shadows had been seen on CCTV. It was the reports of sounds and sightings that I found the most intriguing.

Over the years both staff and patrons have reported seeing the figure of a Victorian lady holding hands with a child. They would walk through the pub without looking up or being aware of their surroundings, before disappearing into the door that led to the cellar below. This was often followed or accompanied by the sound of sobbing children. When anyone built up the courage to go down to the cellar to investigate, they found nobody there.

Soon the stories became folklore, and it was believed it was the ghost of Mary Ann Cotton hiding the bodies of two young victims in the tunnels below. Indeed, there are tunnels that lead from the cellar down to the riverside. Also, Millfield is part of Sunderland that neighbours Pallion where we know she lived. Another fact is that she also worked as nurse in the nearby hospital on Chester Road, so it is possible she would have been in the area before the Ship Isis was opened.

Is the ghostly visitor of the Ship Isis that of notorious serial killer Mary Ann Cotton? I'll let you decide.

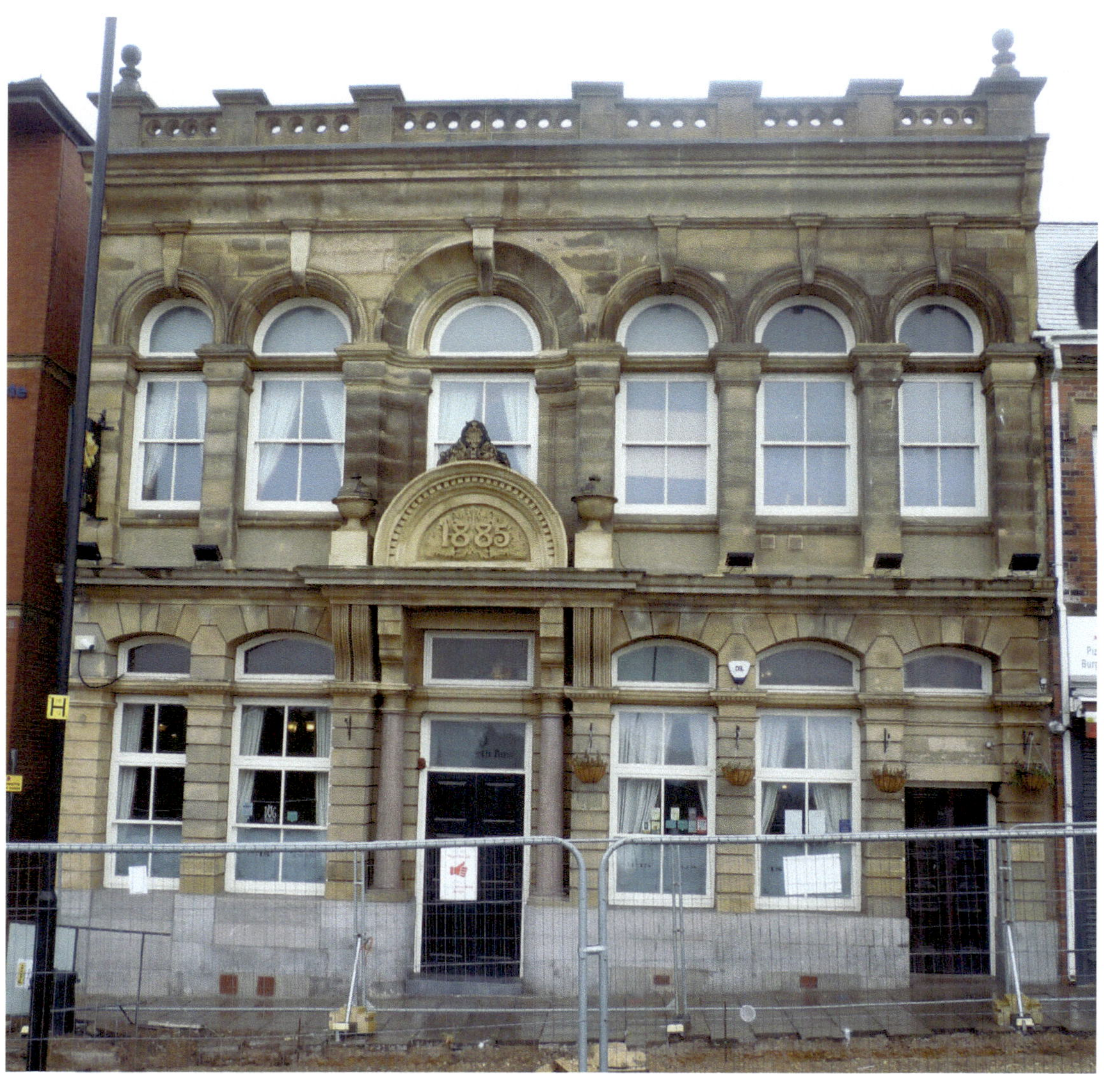

Outside of the pub.

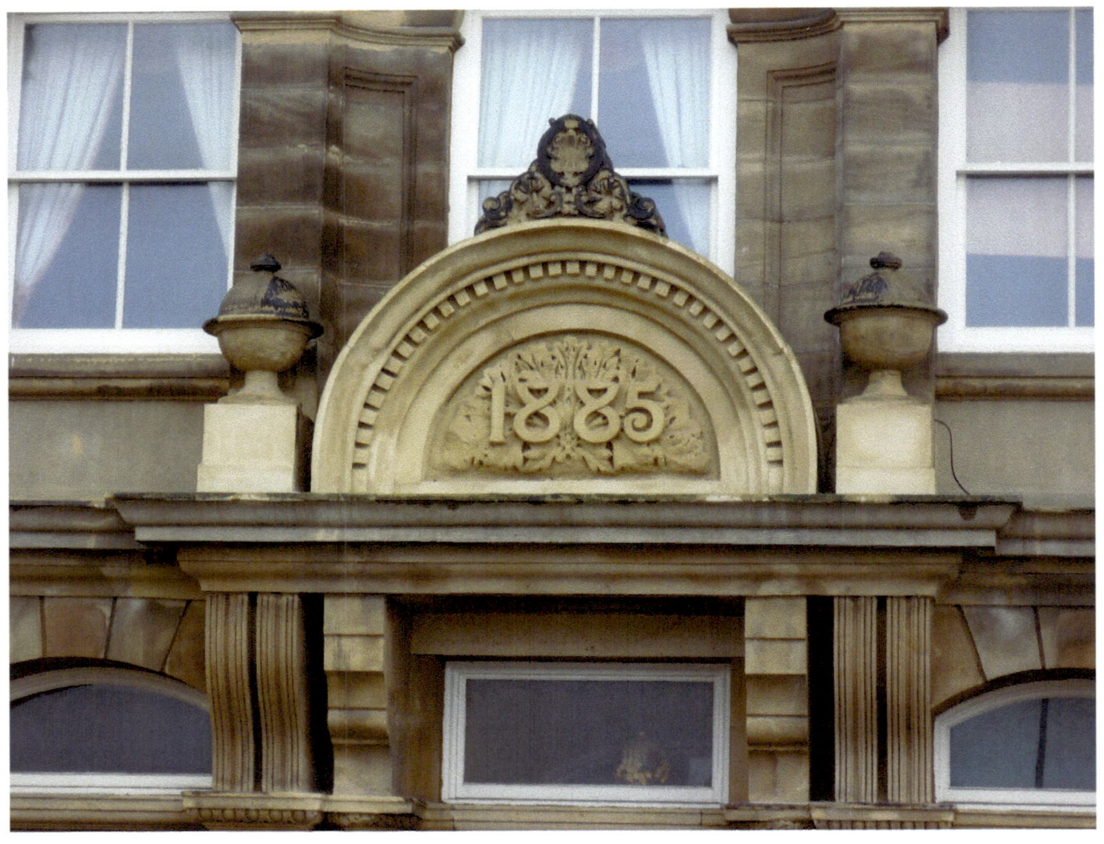

A carving celebrating the opening of the public house.

CHAPTER 16

Doxford House

Doxford House is situated in Silksworth and until as late as the 1960s it was called Silksworth House. Silksworth is an interesting part of Sunderland and lies west of the city centre. We know old Silksworth dates as far back as the Bronze Age as remains of a settlement were unearthed in the area and the hills that surround it. It first appears in the history books at the end of the tenth century when the area was granted to the bishops of Durham. The area then doesn't get mentioned with any note until the eighteenth century when Silksworth House was built by local businessman William Johnson. It took William many years to build his perfect mansion house, having started building work in 1775 and finishing in 1780. The house also included extensive grounds that were turned into impressive gardens.

William died in 1792 and, as he had no family, he left the estate to his lifelong friend Henry Hopper. The estate was then passed through the Hopper family to his nephew Thomas, then his daughter Priscilla. In 1831, Priscilla married an interesting character who is well known in Sunderland's history. She married Mr Willian Beckwith of Thurcroft. William would be remembered for his battles at Waterloo that would see him promoted to general and later, during the late 1850s, he would become the High Sheriff of Durham before moving with his wife to Shropshire in 1890. Interestingly, he added his family's coat of arms above the entrance to the house and after his death was buried in the nearby village of Houghton-le-Spring.

The house was leased to John Craven, who had made his fortune from his company British Ropes. John lived there until his death in 1902 and the Doxford family moved in.

Robert and Charles Doxford had become wealthy from their shipbuilding company that had thrived on the banks of the Wear. Charles bought the lease for land, moved his family into the mansion and was responsible for landscaping the gardens. Charles would live at house until his death in 1935. As his wife had died before him, the estate was left to his son Charles Jr and daughter Aline. Charles Jr moved out of the estate once he had married, and he and his wife moved to Cumbria. Aline stayed on and bought out the lease. She lived on the estate until her death in 1968.

When Aline died she bequeathed the mansion house and its grounds to the Sunderland Corporation for the people of Sunderland to enjoy. In honour of Aline and the importance of her family to Sunderland's heritage and prosperity, the Corporation renamed the building to Doxford House and the surrounding gardens as Doxford Park.

During the two centuries while the house was occupied, the new Silksworth village had sprung up around a new colliery. Silksworth Colliery would mine coal over a century from 1869 to 1971 and the area would thrive with the prosperity from the mine.

Doxford House has many ghost stories, with General Beckwith taking centre stage in many of them. He has been spotted as far back as 1930 where he was always seen near the bottom of the staircase or in the master bedroom. He was also spotted many times when the house became student accommodation in the 1990s. One story was told by two students at the time who described seeing a large man dressed in military garb. He was standing proud in one of the corridors looking upwards. They said he also had a large pistol hanging from his belt. He disappeared as fast as he had appeared, leaving the students puzzled. When they later spoke of the encounter, a number of people told them not to worry about it, as it was General Beckwith and he was often seen in the area.

The face of a woman is also reported to appear at an upstairs window at the back of the house. She is often seen as dusk falls and seems to be staring out over the gardens. It could be the light reflecting onto something in the building or is it Aline Doxford still enjoying the surroundings of the house she loved?

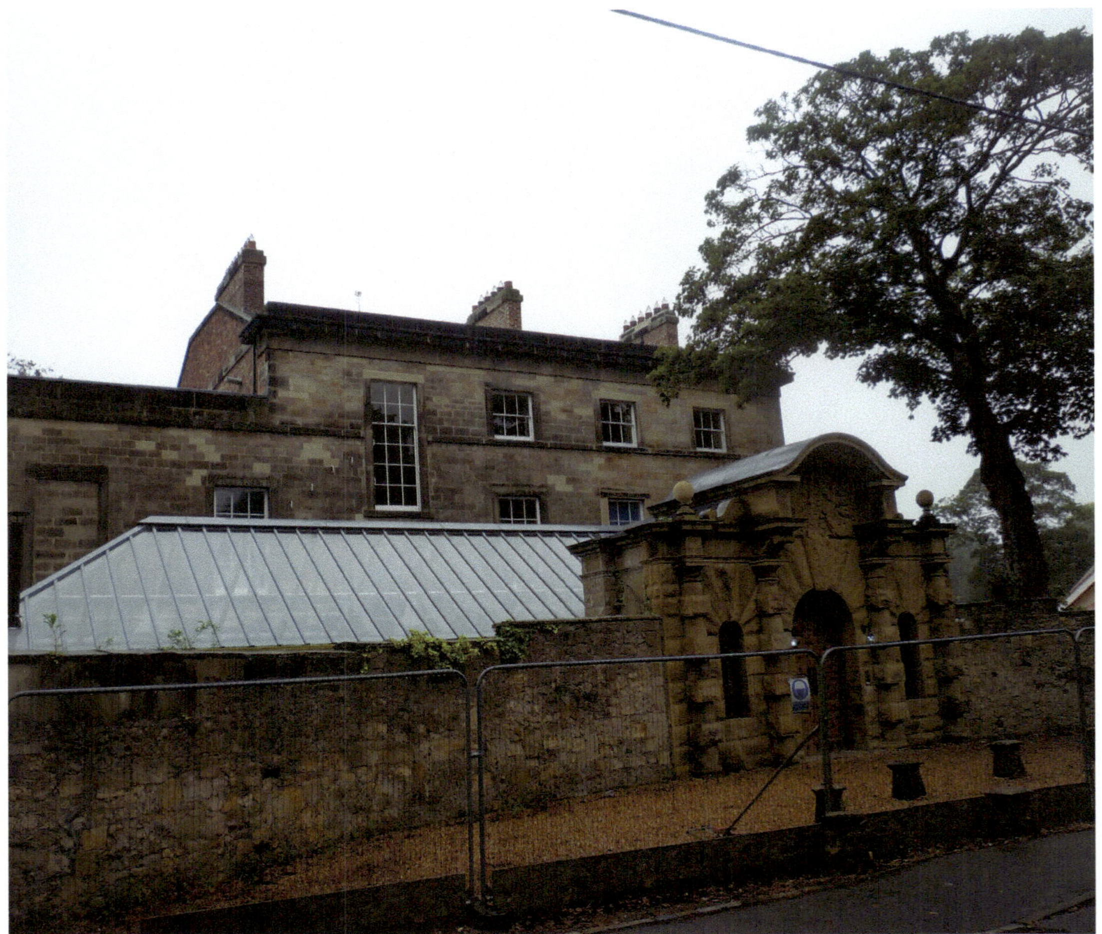

The hall is currently under construction.

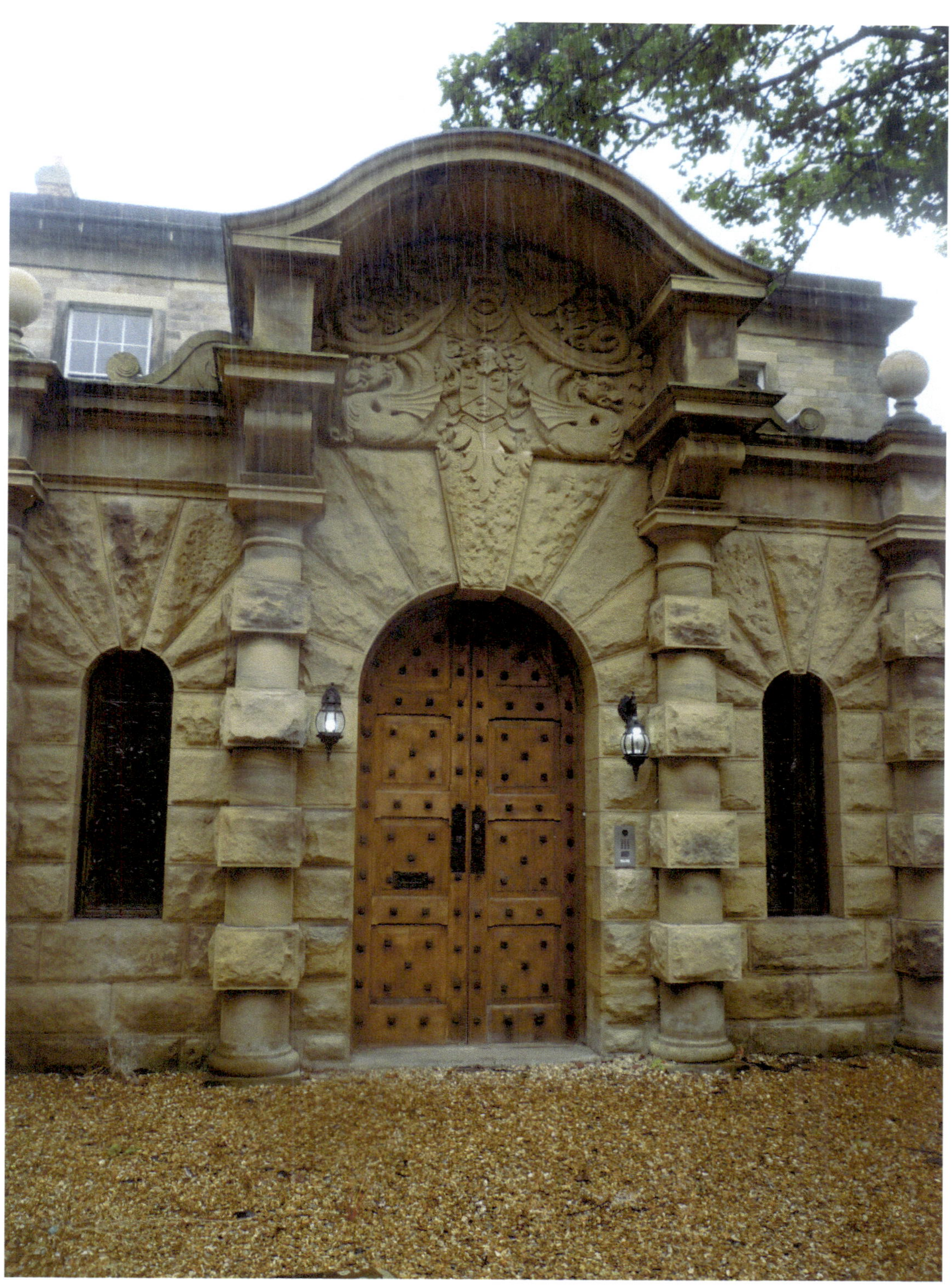

The original gated entrance.

CHAPTER 17

The Academy of Light

The Academy of Light is the training complex built and used by Sunderland Football Club. The academy was built in 2003 and is located on the northern outskirts of the city between Fulwell and Cleadon.

The complex has had its fair share of apparitions and paranormal activity. A dark figure has been spotted in the corridors and across the facility. The sighting of the figure was confirmed by Marcus Stewart in a radio interview during the 2004/05 season. He claimed that he believed the stories were true as Sunderland striker Stephen Elliott had seen it. And it was believed that two of the backroom staff had given chase to a figure that disappeared within the building. Other staff members have confirmed being afraid or uncomfortable for no reason while walking around the building during quiet times of the day and night.

As it is a new building I was quite intrigued at the stories; however, when you look at the surrounding area, it might not be so unbelievable. The academy is built upon the ruins of a seventeenth- or eighteenth-century farmhouse, although it is difficult to find any details in the history books. However, if you walk a few minutes south across the fields you come to an interesting area.

Cut Throat Dene runs along the bottom of the facility. The official story around its name is that it has derived from 'cut through', as in being used as a short cut. Now, I have heard of a 'cut through lane', but why would you say 'cut through the dene'? And cut through to where? I prefer the stories I've been told over the years about the area, although I have to say none of the tales have any researchable facts.

I was told that the name derived from the 1800s as it was a place of many suicides, where the poor souls had taken their lives by cutting their own throats and their ghosts still wander through the wooded area today.

Another story I was told was that of a notorious highwaymen gang that were active across Wearside in the eighteenth century. It was said that the highwaymen would stop the wealthy stagecoaches travelling from London to Scotland or between Durham and Newcastle to rob them of their riches. If the travellers put up a fight or the highwaymen could be identified, they would take the stagecoaches into the woods of Cut Throat Dene and murder the unfortunate passengers by taking a knife to their throats.

If these stories of the area were not enough, there is also another area of note nearby called Dene Lane. Dene Lane is only a few minutes' walk away from the academy and is thought to date back to the eight century as it was a road that the monks would use to travel between the monasteries of Jarrow and Wearmouth. The route would travel north and possibly past the where the academy now stands.

So, could the dark shadow seen by the players and staff of Sunderland Academy be that of the inhabitants of the old farmhouse, a lawless highwayman or a monk that is angered by his path being blocked by the modern building?

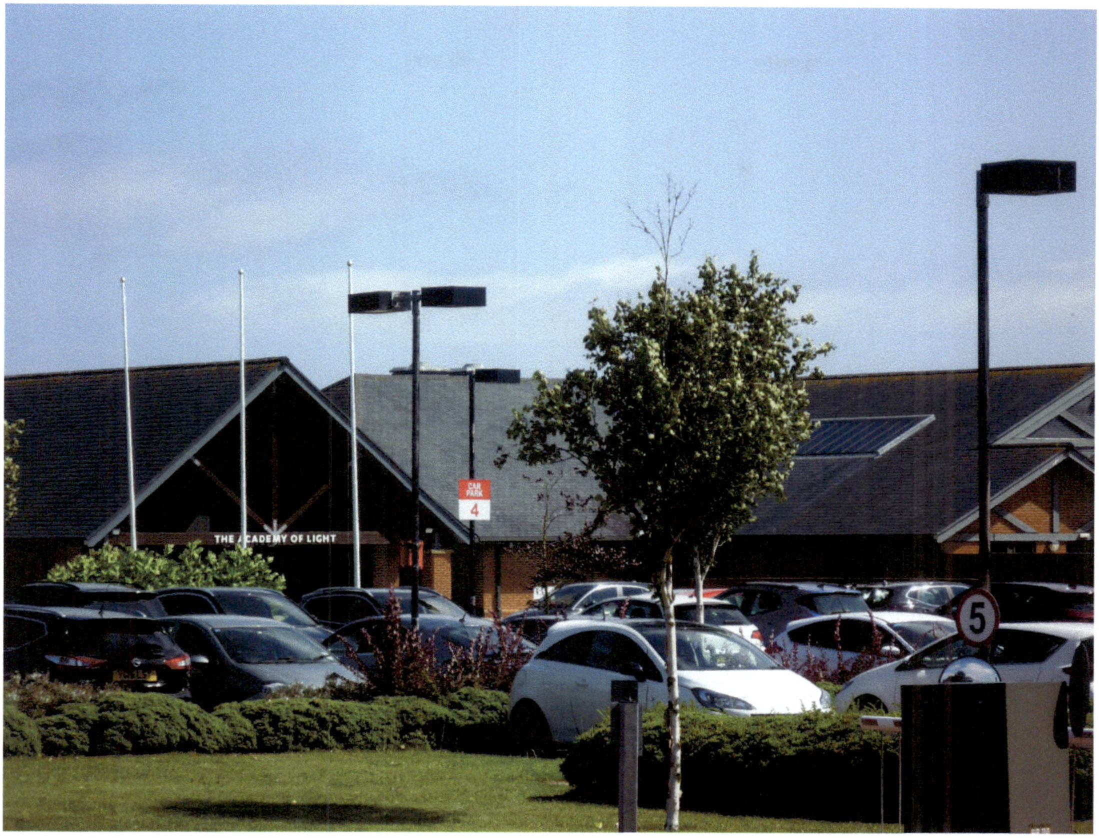

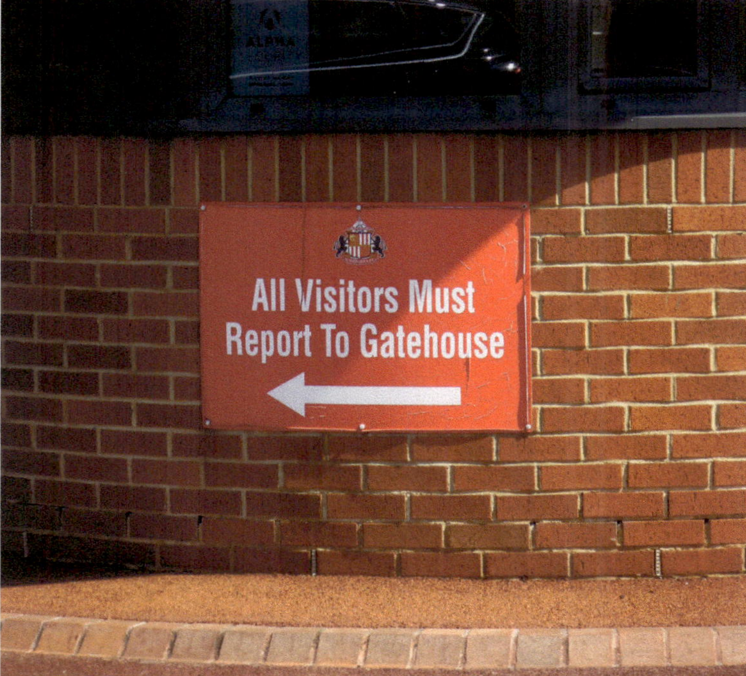

Above: The Academy of Light.

Right: Entrance to the facility.

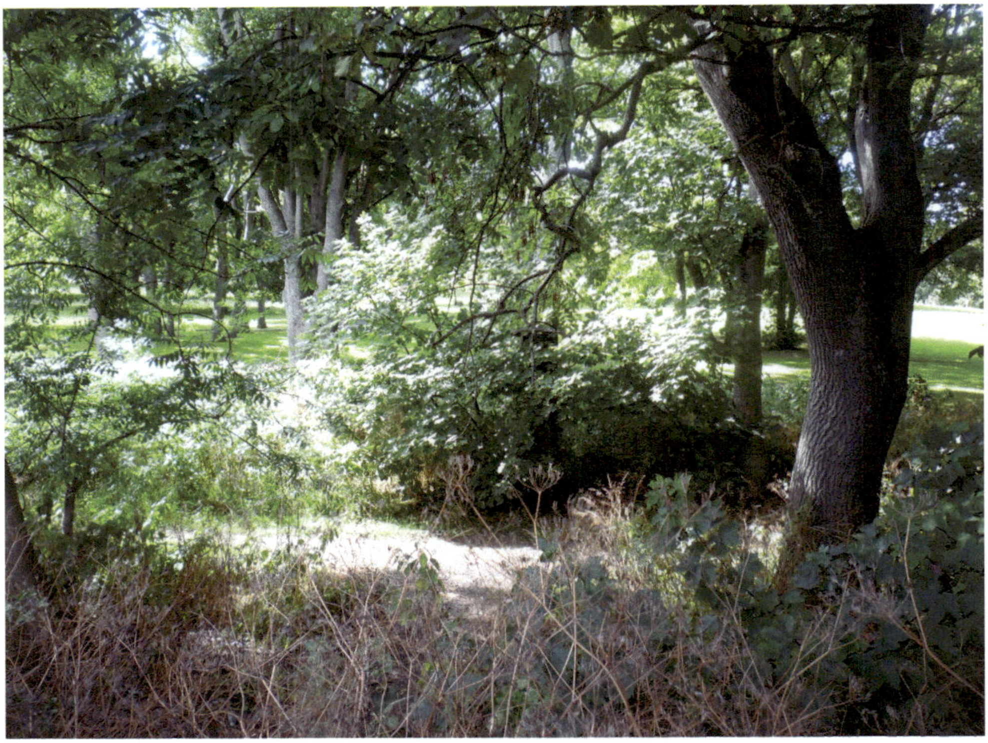

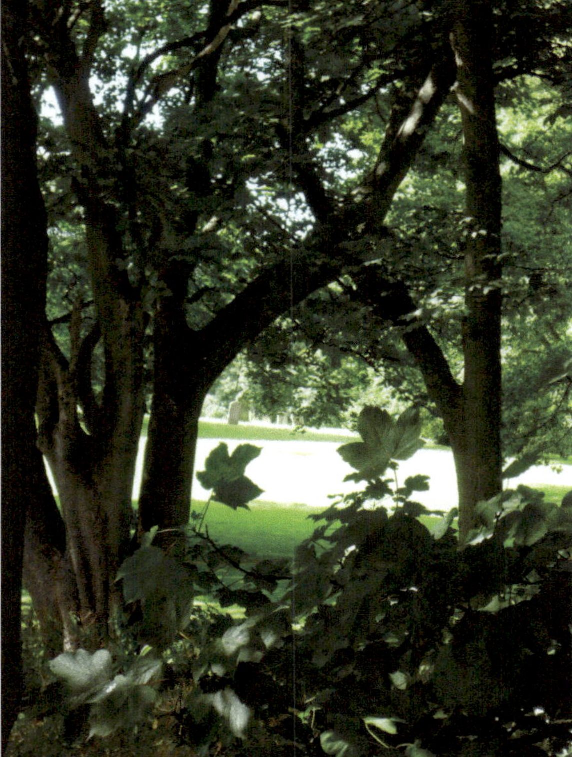

Above: Cut Throat Dene.

Left: The Dene with the cemetery in the background.

CHAPTER 18

Peat's Hall

South of the town centre is a suburb of Sunderland called Herrington. Herrington has a fascinating history and was once four small farming communities that were originally part of County Durham. The areas were called East, West, New and Middle Herrington and the small hamlets date back over 800 years when the area belonged to the monks of St Cuthbert.

As with most parts of the region, the locals turned their backs on farming in the nineteenth century as pit shafts were sunk all around the Durham and Sunderland area. Herrington was no different, as Herrington Colliery was opened in 1874, located in the New village area. The colliery would continue to produce the 'black gold' until it's closure in 1985.

As Sunderland grew in the twentieth century, the four areas were joined by housing estates built for modern living and Herrington became one of them, before joining the borough of Sunderland.

The Herrington area was one of wealth dating back to Henry VIII's reign when a family named Robinson built Herrington Hall. Over the years the Robinsons became well known, with one of the daughters marrying Robert Burns' son and another marrying Robert Surtees. Over the centuries the estate changed hands until 1958 when the hall was demolished as it had become unsafe and the then owners NCB decided it was not viable for repair.

However, this building rich in history is not the one I'm going to concentrate on, as not far down the lane was another building called Herrington House, which would become better known as Peats Hall.

Little is known of Peats Hall in its earlier days. We do know it was built in the early 1700s by local squire Matthew Smith and his wife Jane. The Smiths only had one child, a daughter named after her mother, and as a family they don't feature prominently in Sunderland's history. The only mention in the early days is when Matthew and his daughter refused to pay a toll and were then taken to court, where they were fined.

Mrs Smith died before her husband and then in 1793 Matthew died at home, leaving the estate and hall to his only heir, his daughter Jane.

Jane continued to live at the hall and become to get a reputation as a miser with her money. She had been caught thieving around Sunderland on many occasions, much to the locals' surprise, as she had wealth from the estate she had bequeathed. I suppose today she would be seen as a kleptomaniac and an eccentric.

Sir Robert Peat was introduced to Jane Smith by a mutual friend and proposed marriage to her. Sir Robert had problems with gambling and saw an opportunity to marry the rich, older woman as a way to support his luxurious lifestyle. Although becoming a dame excited Jane, she declined Robert's initial advances and it was rumoured she had told him that she would never marry while Herrington House still stood. Herrington House didn't stand for much longer, though, as a fatal night in 1815 would witness one of the longest unsolved murders in Sunderland.

On 28 August 1815, a housemaid called Isabella Young had been working for Lady Jane as the housekeeper. Lady Jane had been away for the week collecting the rent from her tenants and, as she moaned about the costs of lighting and heating, Isabella would work through the day and return to her home at night-time. However, as her mistress was due home the next day, Isabella was to stay there overnight readying the building for her return. Sometime in the early hours of the morning a local man that lived nearby was woken to dancing lights at his windows. When he looked out, he could see Herrington House was on fire. He ran into the village, raising the alarm.

Three men ran to the house, knowing that Isabella was still inside. They rushed inside and found her face down in a passageway. Picking her up, they carried her out of the house and sat her down out of the way of the fire, but it was too late as she was already dead. What startled the men was that she had been untouched by the fire and smoke, but her head and face were unrecognisable. A doctor was called from Sunderland, and he confirmed that poor Isabella had been bludgeoned to death before the fire. She had horrific injuries to her head and face.

It soon became known that Isabella's murder seemed to be a robbery gone wrong. Whether the burglars thought the house would be empty or Isabella had disturbed them by mistake, we will never know.

On her return to her home, it was said Lady Jane was more concerned with her house and the valuables that had been stolen rather that the plight of her unfortunate housemaid.

The murderers of Isabella were never found. Three men were accused, but were released as there was no firm evidence. The house was never rebuilt as there was little left of the charred remains.

Lady Jane did go on to marry Sir Robert Peat in the November of the same year. She initially moved to London before the marriage became a farce and she returned to Sunderland. Her husband, although twenty years younger, died five years before her, as Lady Jane Peat died at the age of ninety-one.

Two ghosts have been spotted on many occasions in Herrington Park near to where Peat's Hall once stood. The first is of an old woman who appears stooped as she walks around the trees and field looking for something on the ground. Described as wearing Georgian-era clothing and a hat she has been heard muttering, 'Don't tell Lady Peat!' Is it the spirit of Jane Smith still looking for her valuables after all of this time?

The second ghost story involves seeing a young woman sitting on the field near to where the house was. She is described as wearing a white petticoat and sobbing into her hands. The descriptions perfectly match the way Isabella Young would have looked and dressed. But if you see her don't go too close because when you get close enough to speak to her she pulls away her hands to reveal a bloody and disfigured face before screaming.

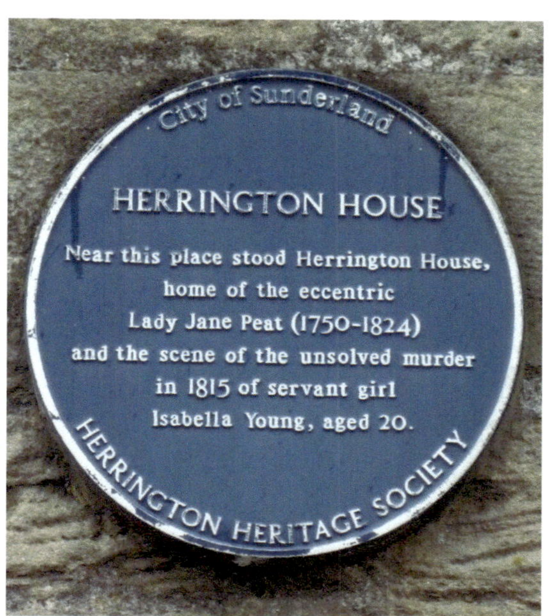

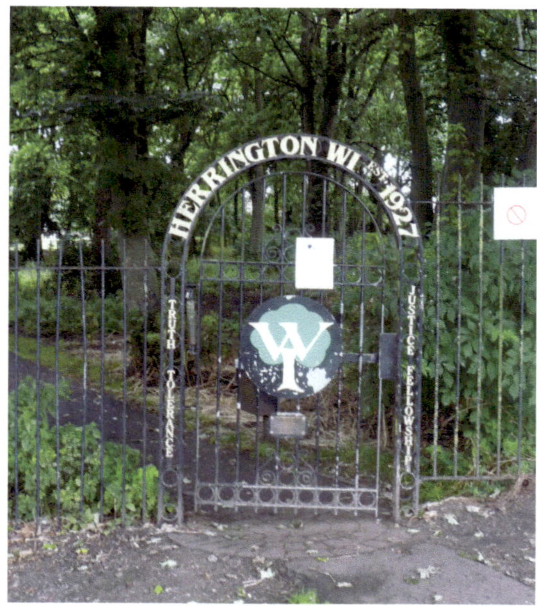

Above left: A blue plaque celebrating the site of Peat's Hall, or Herrington House as it is better known.

Above right: The hall's land is now a public park.

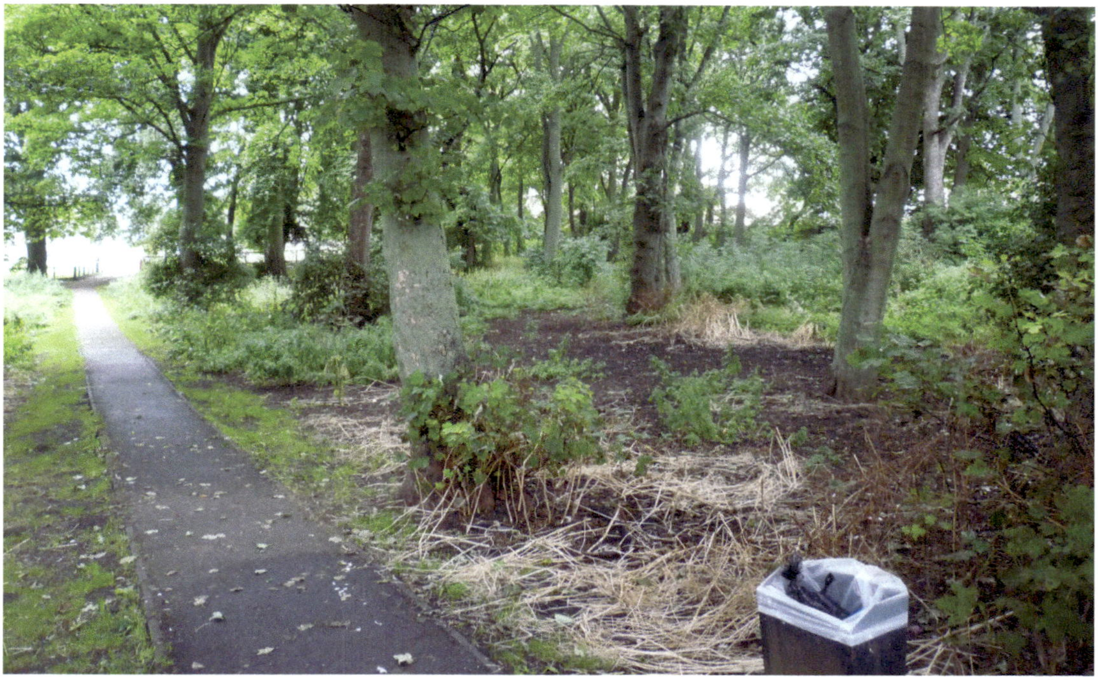

The area where a young lady is seen.

CHAPTER 19

Prospect Row Mission

This is the first of two stories that involve the poor Victorian children of Sunderland and two buildings that are very close to one another.

Prospect Row Mission is situated in Hendon, near to the Town Moor part of the old town, and was built by the church in 1885. The building is historic as it was the first community building to have a modern emergency exit door that opened outwards as demanded by the changes in building laws after the great tragedy of the nearby Victoria Hall. In 1883, a magic show at the hall went dramatically wrong when it led to over 1,000 children rushing out of the building at the same time. The doors only opened inwards and a huge crush ensued, leaving 183 boys and girls dead. The poor souls have a memorial in Mowbray Park as the Victoria Hall was bombed and demolished during the Second World War. The disaster led to the invention of the emergency exit and push bars.

Prospect Row Mission was opened for the poor children in the area and would offer them food, shelter and education. It would also give them a sense of belonging and a path to religion as most missions or ragged schools belonged to the church. The mission continued its work for decades and in more modern times was used as a community centre, boxing club and gymnasium.

A lot of stories of ghosts in the building are related to children, with boys and girls spotted wearing old-fashioned clothes or being of a dirty appearance. Children's laughter and footsteps were often heard in the gym area. It was said that the hanging punch bags would swing back and forth on their own, as if they had been bumped into or pushed. However, the most common story I have heard is that of singing. It's always described as children's voices singing and the songs sound like hymns that are sung in church.

CHAPTER 20

Sunderland Boys' Orphanage

Only a couple of minutes' walk from the Prospect Row Mission is another children's home. Originally called the Sunderland Orphan Asylum, this stunning building opened its doors to its inmates in 1861.

The orphanage was home to fifty boys at any given time and they were all orphans of sailors who came to Sunderland from all over the country. Depending on who's recollections you listen to, they seemed to be well fed and looked after, although some boys hated the place and many tried to abscond over the years.

The boys all had to dress in sailor's uniforms and spent their youth learning the trades needed to work at sea, whether that be on commercial vessels or joining the Royal Navy. Indeed, the orphanage has an excellent record for producing military sailors and captains that went on to earn honours during both world wars.

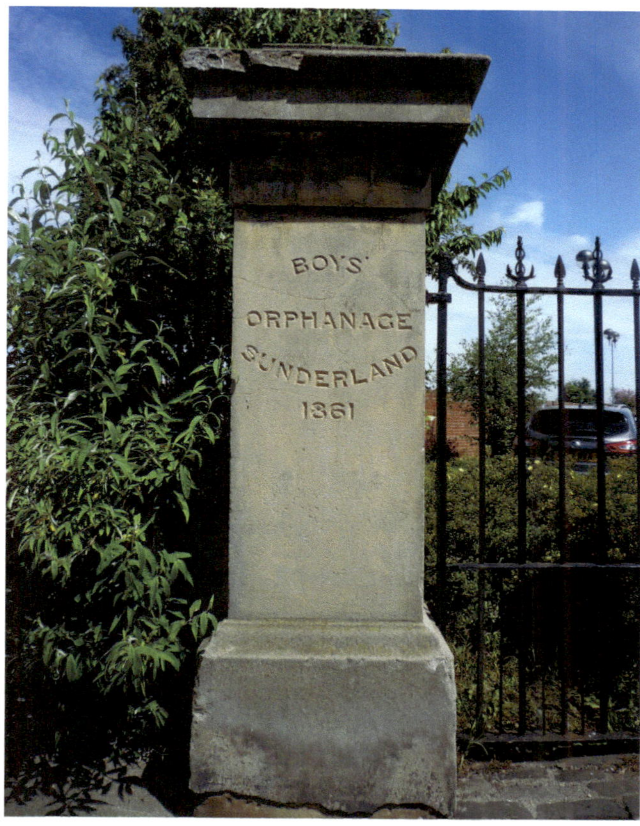

Outside the Sunderland Boys' Orphanage.

Obviously, many of the ghost stories surrounding the orphanage are the sightings of boys in and outside. Many of the sightings outside are of boys dressed in uniform running around or voices laughing loudly, only for there to be no one there when you look out of the windows onto grounds.

Another story is of the crying boy in the tower. It is said he is seen looking out of the windows on the second floor and is a sad sight to see. He is believed to be one of the orphans hoping that it is all a mistake and is waiting for his dad to return from sea and come to take him home.

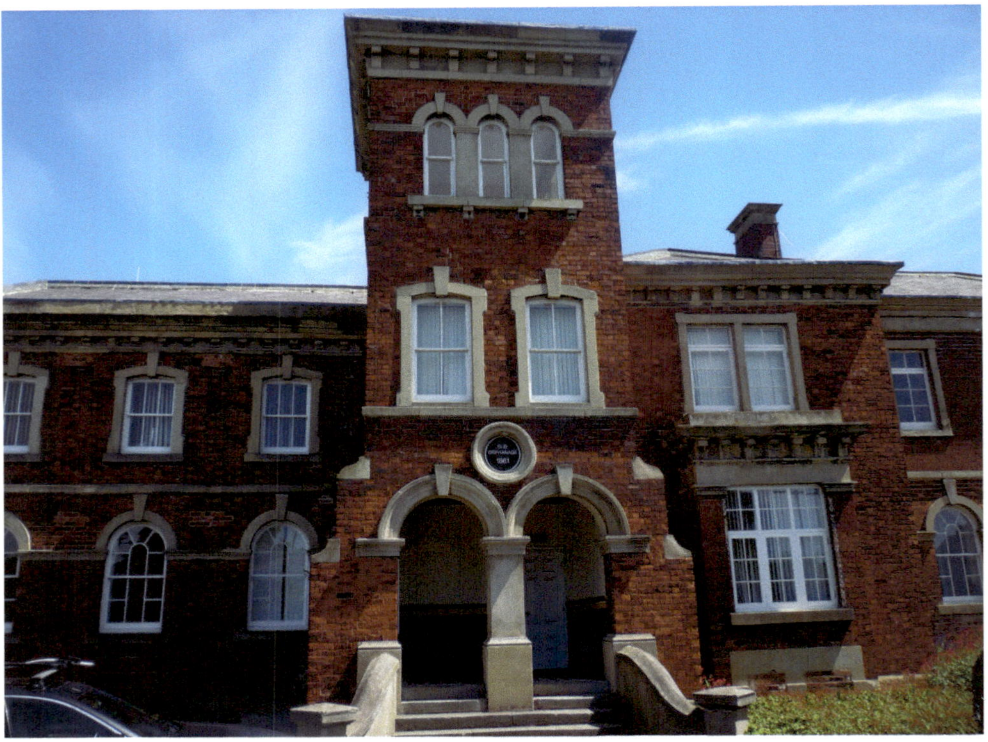

The second-floor tower is where a young boy is sighted.

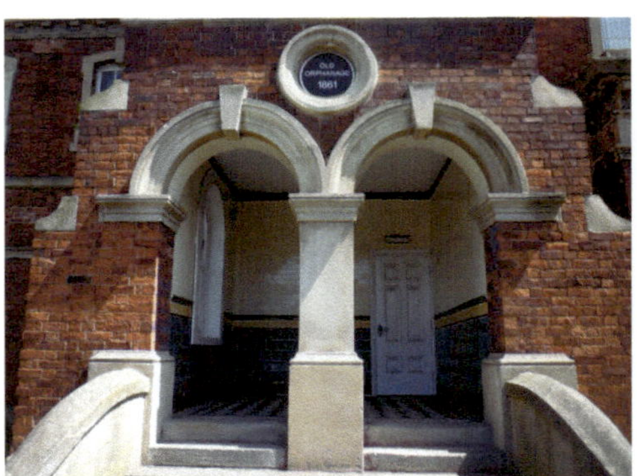

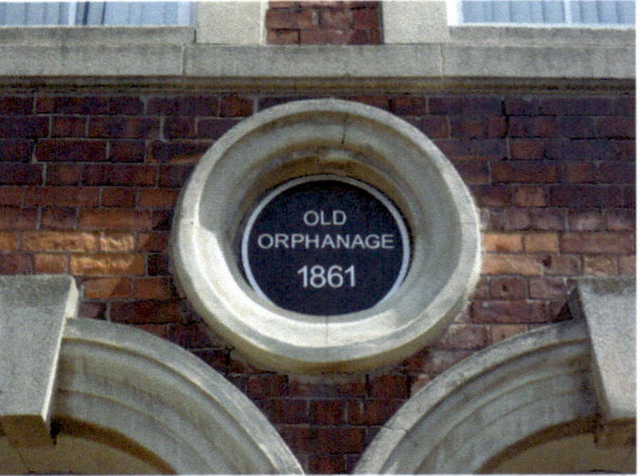

Above left: The entrance.

Above right: Established in 1861.

CHAPTER 21

St Peter's Church

St Peter's Church is the oldest building in Sunderland. Still standing proud in the centre of Monkwearmouth, the church is where Sunderland first began.

The church started its life as a monastery dating back to AD 674 when it was twinned with St Paul's Church in Jarrow, a town north of Sunderland, creating the Monkwearmouth-Jarrow Abbey. The church was built by the order of Benedict Bishop on land given to him by King Ecgfirth of Northumbria.

The monasteries would be home to the Venerable Bede. Bede grew up between the two monasteries and was recognised for his incredible intellect as a scholar, writer and educator. He would become known as 'the Father of British History' or 'the First Historian' after writing *The Ecclesiastical History of the English People* – a masterpiece of his time.

Over the next 900 years the abbey would suffer. During the late eighth century, England was raided by Vikings and Monkwearmouth-Jarrow Abbey was one of their first mainland targets. The area was ransacked, and the abbey lay in ruins. During the eleventh and twelfth centuries, the Normans rebuilt the abbey and the monasteries thrived until the arrival of Henry VIII, who decided to burn down the monasteries and dissolve the church before introducing the Church of England so he could marry Anne Boleyn.

Unfortunately, nothing of the abbey remains today, but the church still stands. The front porch and west wall are the only original parts of the building that was so lovingly built by Benedict Biscop. The other parts of the church were added mostly through the thirteenth and fourteenth centuries, with additional restoration work at the end of the eighteenth century. With over 1,300 years of history within the walls of the church and surrounding area, it comes as no surprise that the area has a wealth of ghost stories and reports of paranormal activity.

Dark figures are spotted within the grounds of St Peter's. They are described as tall and hooded and are often seen shuffling along the paths. The figures are often accompanied by the sound of male voices chanting. The figures then disappear through the walls into the church. The sound of chanting has been heard coming from inside the church when the church is locked and empty. The apparitions are thought to be the monks of Monkwearmouth returning to their spiritual home.

Apparitions of Vikings have also been spotted in and around the church area. These spirits are usually reported during bad weather, when there is thunder and lightening or heavy rainfall. I have no reasonable explanation as to why the Vikings only appear during storms, perhaps that was the weather when they raided Britain and attacked Monkwearmouth.

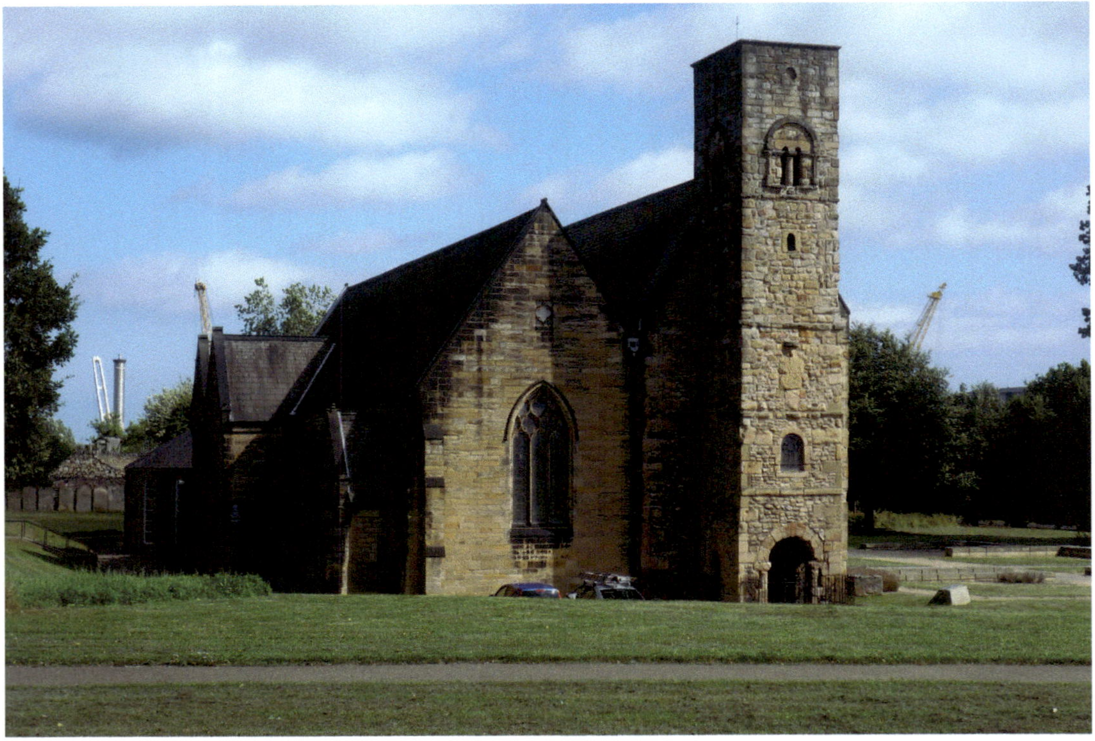

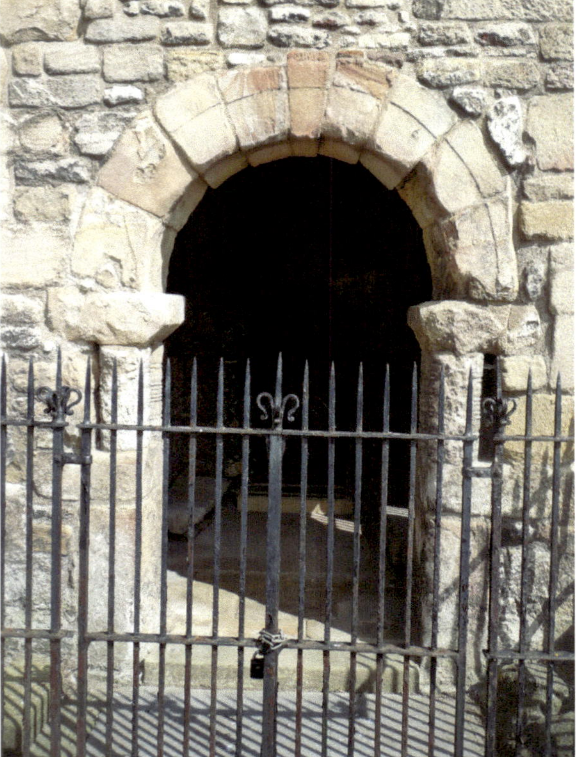

Above: St Peter's Church.

Left: The oldest part of the church.

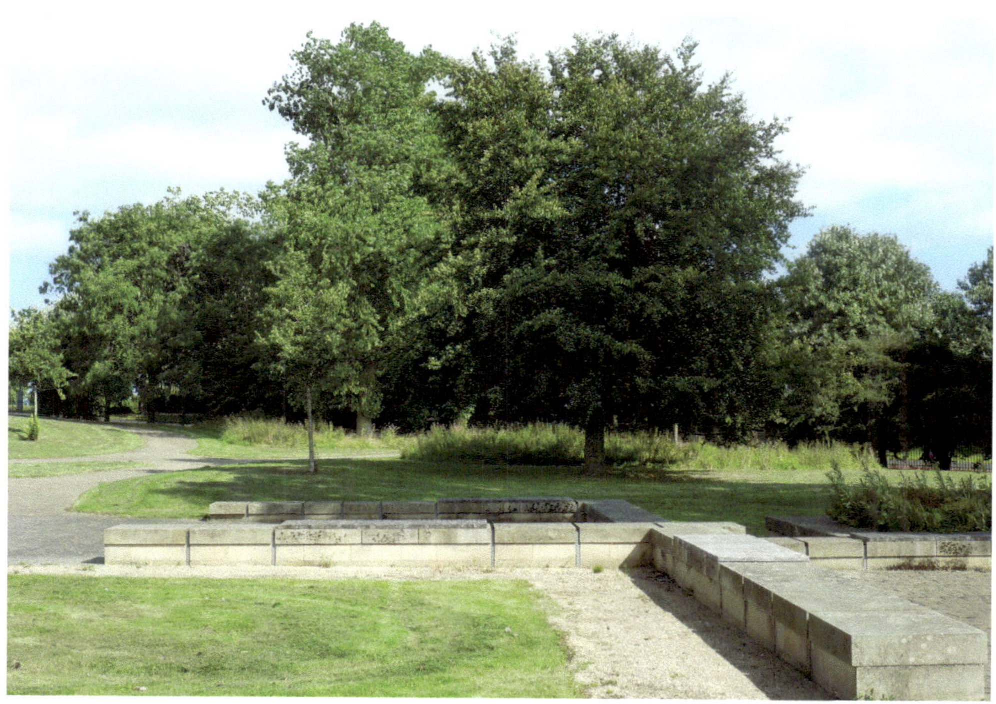

The grounds of the church hold ghostly monks, and Vikings have also been reported.

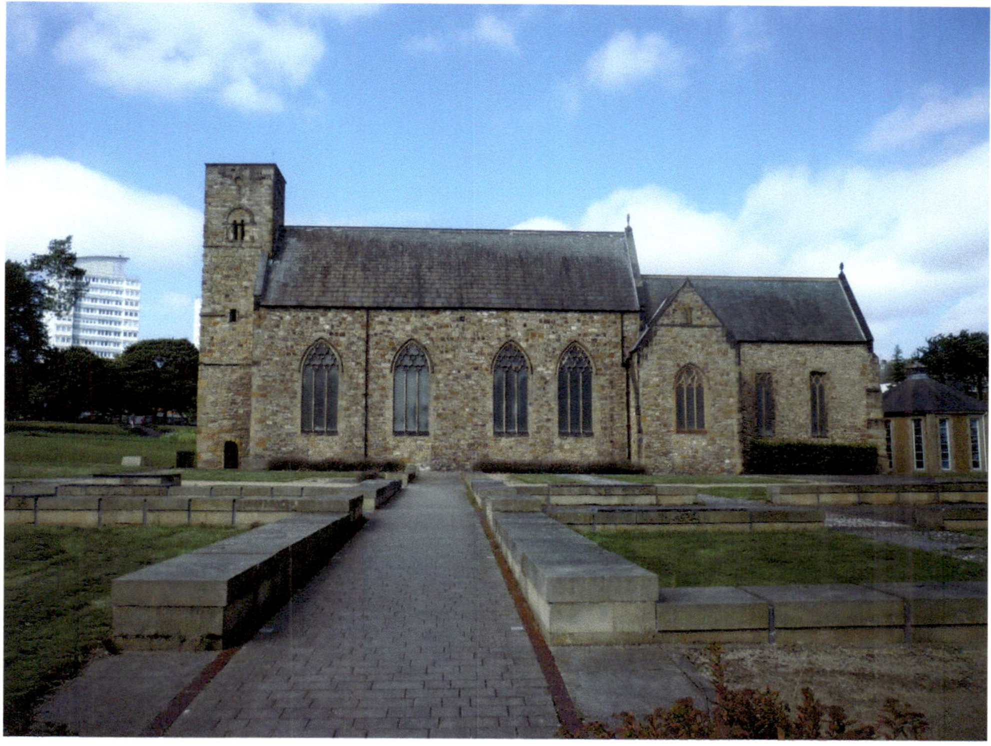

Monkwearmouth Monastery is marked out in front of the church.

CHAPTER 22

Fulwell Mill

Fulwell has a wealth of history attached to this northern suburb of Sunderland. We know from old maps and history books that it was the site of a manor house in the late eighteenth century. The house belonged to a gentleman called Robert Atkinson and was located at the east end of today's Station Road, near to the Blue Bell pub. The Blue Bell has its own history, with it being the site of a coaching inn that was attached to many stories of smugglers during the 1800s.

The village grew around its quarries and became a very wealthy area during the Victorian era. The quarries in the surrounding hills have one of the strangest of stories I have been told, and that is of the 'Fulwell Giant'.

In 1759, while digging limestone out of the quarry, the quarrymen came across four large stones. The stones were not natural with the lay of the land, so they lifted them out of the way. Lying in the ground was the human skeleton of a man, but not an ordinary man, as he measured 9 feet and 6 inches. Also buried next to him were two Roman coins. It was believed he was a Roman soldier who had died in the area and was given a respectable burial. I must admit, if the Romans had soldiers of this size, it is no wonder they won as many battles as they did!

The hills are also home to Fulwell Mill. Standing proud looking over Fulwell, the limestone mill was opened in 1808 by Joseph Swan, the man we have to thank for the electric light bulb. The mill would be home to Sunderland millers for over 100 years until it finally stopped turning in 1956. During the latter part of the twentieth century the mill started to deteriorate as it remained empty and unused. Thankfully, a number of charities, with the help of the city council, have now restored the building – complete with sails.

The ghost that is reported at the mill is said to be a man on the sails of the mill, or he is spotted laying on the ground near to the building. Like the Vikings in the previous chapter, he is seen more often on stormy days and nights. The sightings have even led to phone calls to the local police station from people saying they have seen a man hanging onto the sails of the mill screaming for his life.

If you ever witness this strange phenomena, it is probably the ghost of William Wren. William was a time-served miller that lived in Sunderland, and during the storms of 1834 he climbed the windmill to try and repair the sails. Unfortunately, the safety ropes that he was attached to snapped and he was thrown to the ground with force. When help arrived, his injuries were fatal, and he died where he had landed. It is thought that it is his spirit that returns to the windmill to this day.

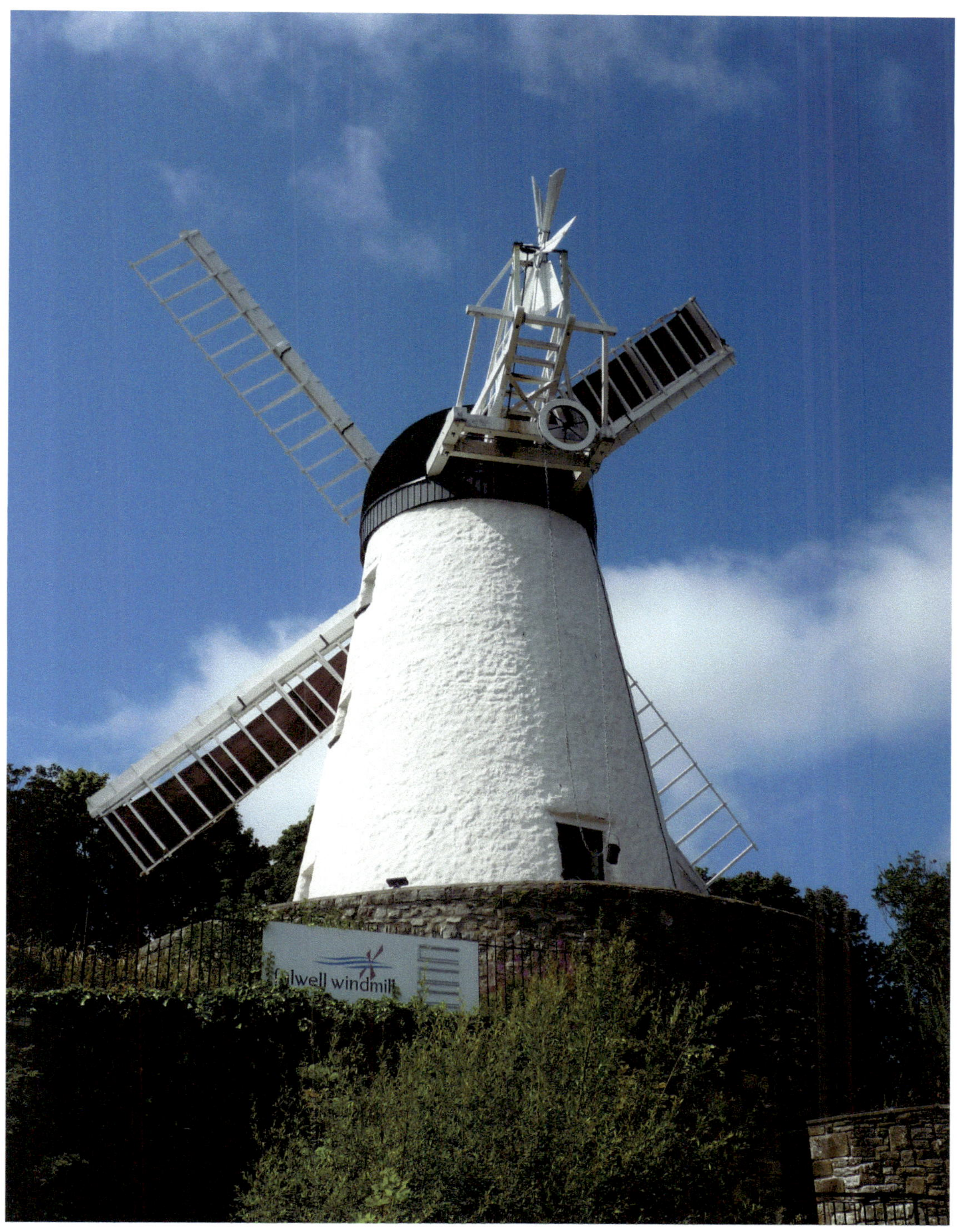

The newly painted Fulwell Mill.

CHAPTER 23

Spottee's Cave

To most people when I mention Roker Park they think 'Oh no, here he goes again waffling on about football', as most people associate the park with the football club due to it being their home for ninety-nine years before they moved to the Stadium of Light. However, I'm not talking about that Roker Park, but the recreational park that leads onto Roker Beach.

Now, the recreational park is home to one of the oldest and most unusual ghost stories I have come across. I remember being a teenager and hearing the grandparents and parents of friends saying, 'If ya didn't behave, auld Spottee will get ya.' As I didn't grow up in Sunderland, I would just look, baffled, before moving on to whichever mischief we were up to.

Later in life, I had forgot all about it until I was in the Colliery Tavern before the match. Sunderland had a terrible run when one of the older gentlemen said, 'It's that bloody Spottee givin' us bloody bad luck', and everyone started laughing. As this was a time before the internet, I waited for the pub to become a bit less crowded and sat next to the elderly gentleman and asked him who Spottee was. In his own words he went on to tell me the following, in a strong northern accent:

Whey lad, wheneva owt gans wrang in Sunderland, especially with the lads and the futbal, Spottee gets the blame. When we were bairns and we used to act up, me ma would tell is we'd get a clip arood the lug or she'd hoy wu ootside and Spottee would come and get wu. He'll tek us doon his cave in Roker and he'll make us clean his hoose before hoying ya on a boat. Poor bugger has been deed and buried for years, but it woked mind ya.

For the readers outside of the North East, I'll translate:

You know what? Whenever anything goes wrong in Sunderland, especially with the football team, Spottee gets the blame. When we were children and we misbehaved, my mam would tell us we'd get smacked or she would throw us outside and Spottee would come and take us away to his cave in Roker, where he'll make us clean his house and then put us on a boat that would take us away. The poor man has been dead and buried for years, but the threats worked.

After thanking him I decided to research who this ghostly spectre was. Spottee was a well-known figure around Roker Beach and Park in the late eighteenth century and the story about him differs depending on which old wives' tale you read.

Most of the tales say that Spottee was a French sailor that was shipwrecked onto Roker Beach and found shelter in the cave, which he made his home. As he couldn't speak English, the locals were terrified of him and he was branded a lunatic. People wouldn't go near him. His nickname came from the shirts he would wear.

Then the various tales start to differ. It was said that he lived as a hermit and made ends meet by begging and doing odd jobs for the local businesses, which were mostly farms or fishermen at that time. He never integrated into the local community and spent the rest of his days as a lonely figure in and around his cave.

Another popular story is a bit more macabre. It is said that Spottee's Cave had a tunnel that led down to rocky cliffs of the North Sea, and he would go out at night-time at set fires on the rocks to lure ships to their doom. Spottee would then sit on the beach and wait for the barrels and chests from the ships to wash ashore, giving no regard to the poor sailors that lost their lives. Although it has to be said that there is no evidence to suggest this was the case, and as of yet there has been no tunnel or cave found full of Spottee's treasure.

Whatever the true story is about Spottee, there does seem to have been a character running around Roker Park and his figure is still spotted today. He is often seen running around the park near to his cave. He has also been seen disappearing into the cave through the closed door that has now been put into place by the council. Poor Spottee's ghost has even been blamed for the dark apparitions that were reported at the Academy and Stadium of Light that I wrote about earlier in this book (see page 56).

Interestingly, a ghost story of the beaches and cliffs of Sunderland towards Whitburn is of a figure that stands near a bright light or fire looking out to the sea on foggy nights, before disappearing as fast as it appears. Could this be Spottee again, still trying to lure ships and boats to a rocky end?

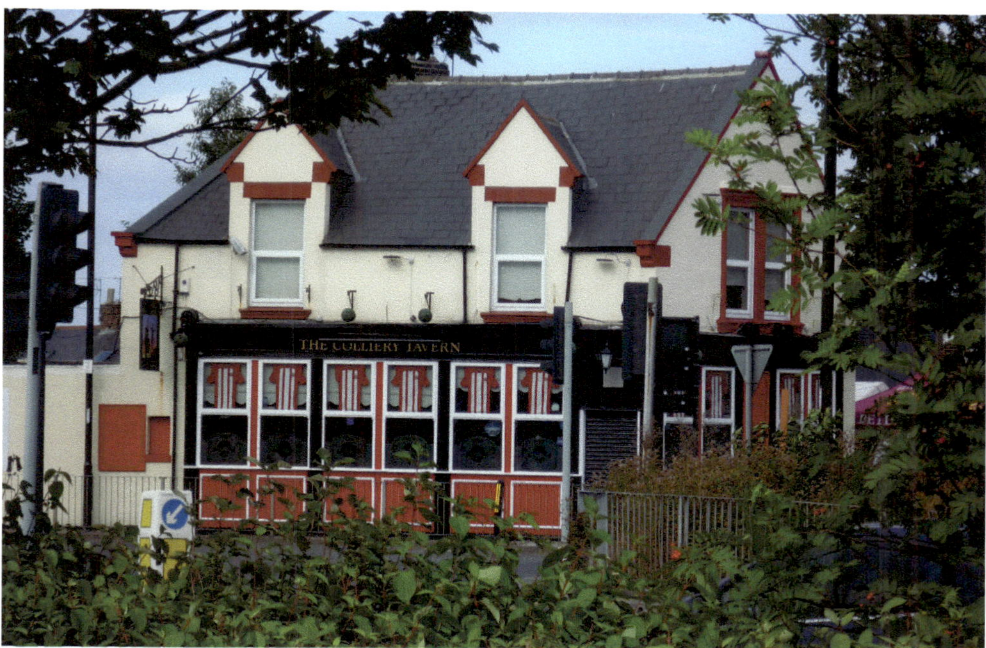

The Colliery tavern, where I was told the story of Spottee.

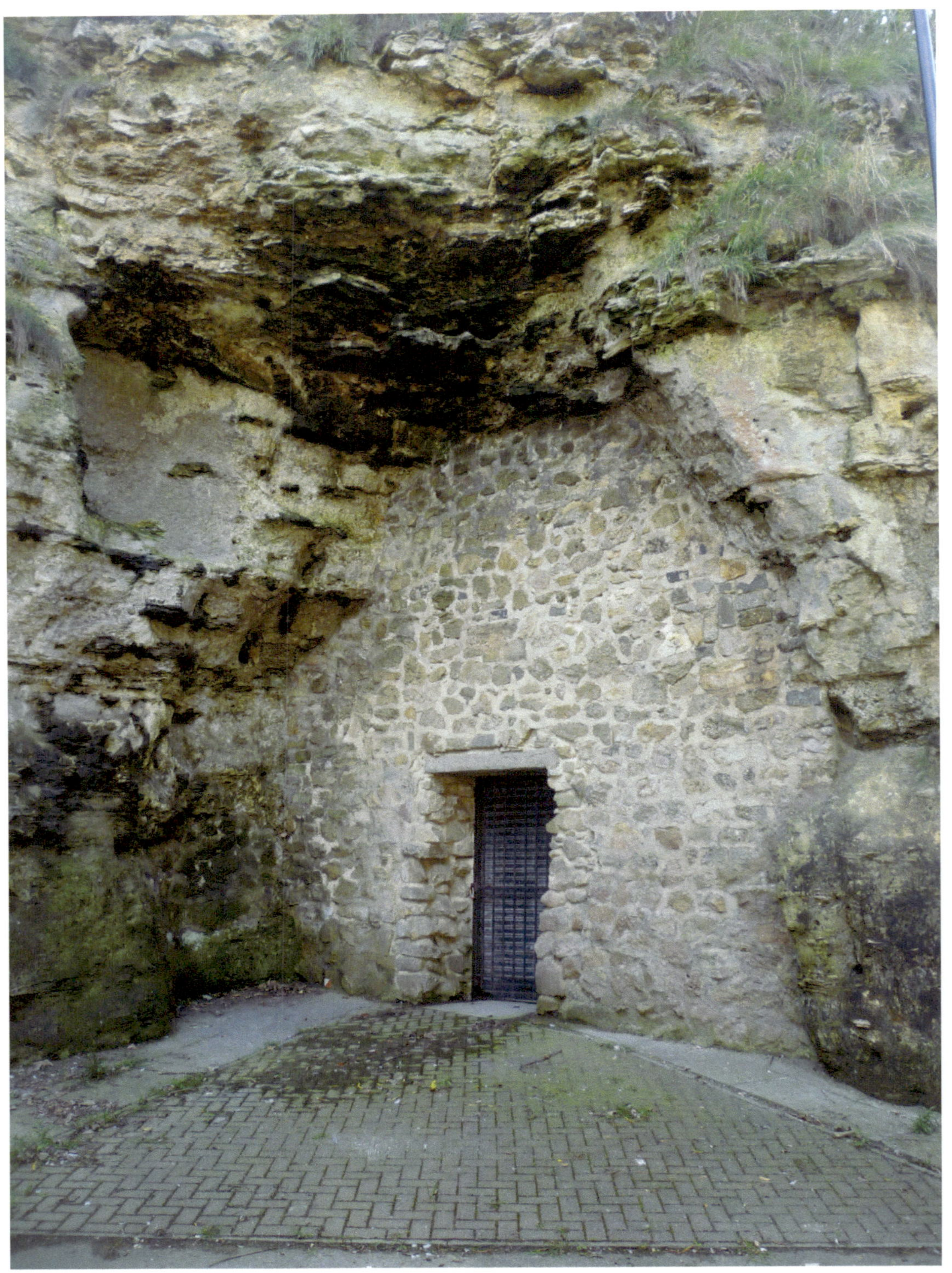

Spottee's Cave, near to Roker Beach.

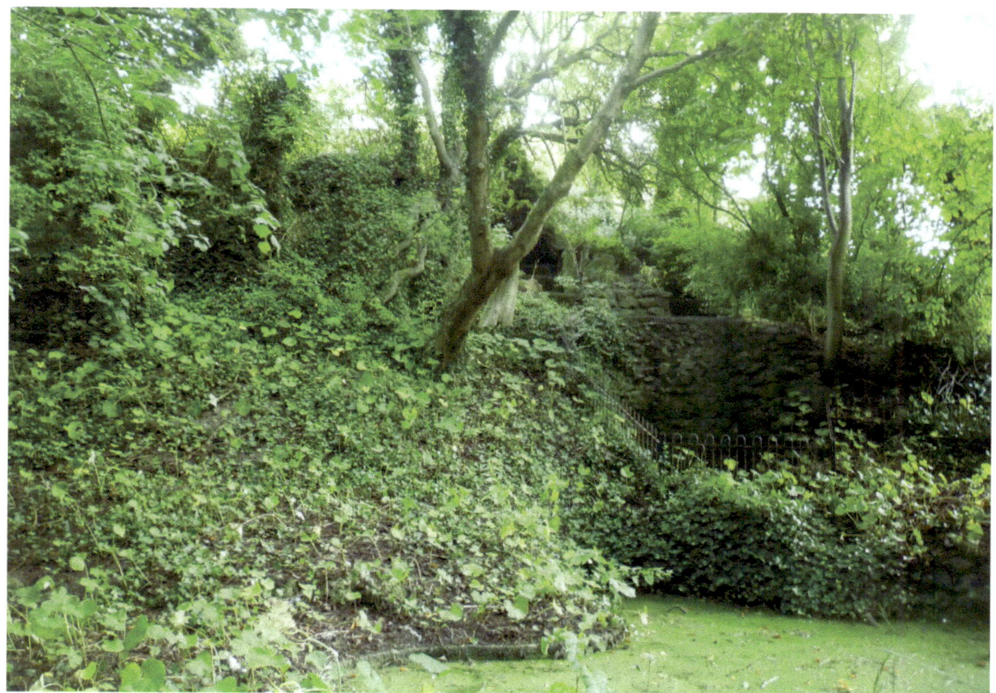

Roker Park, where Spottee is sighted.

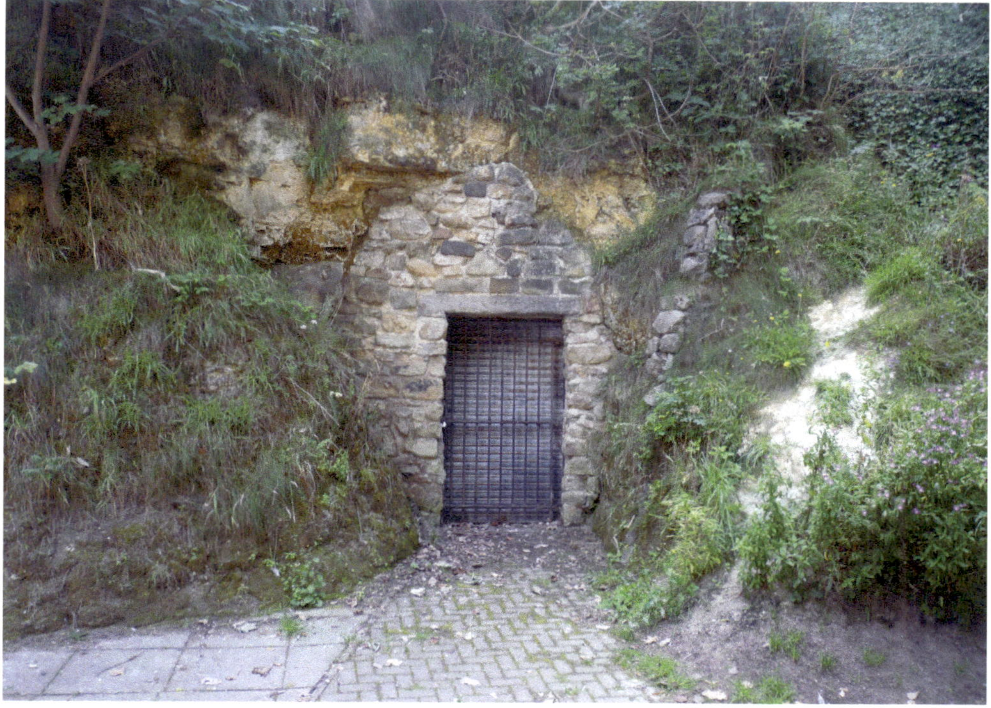

The cliffs are dotted with small caves.

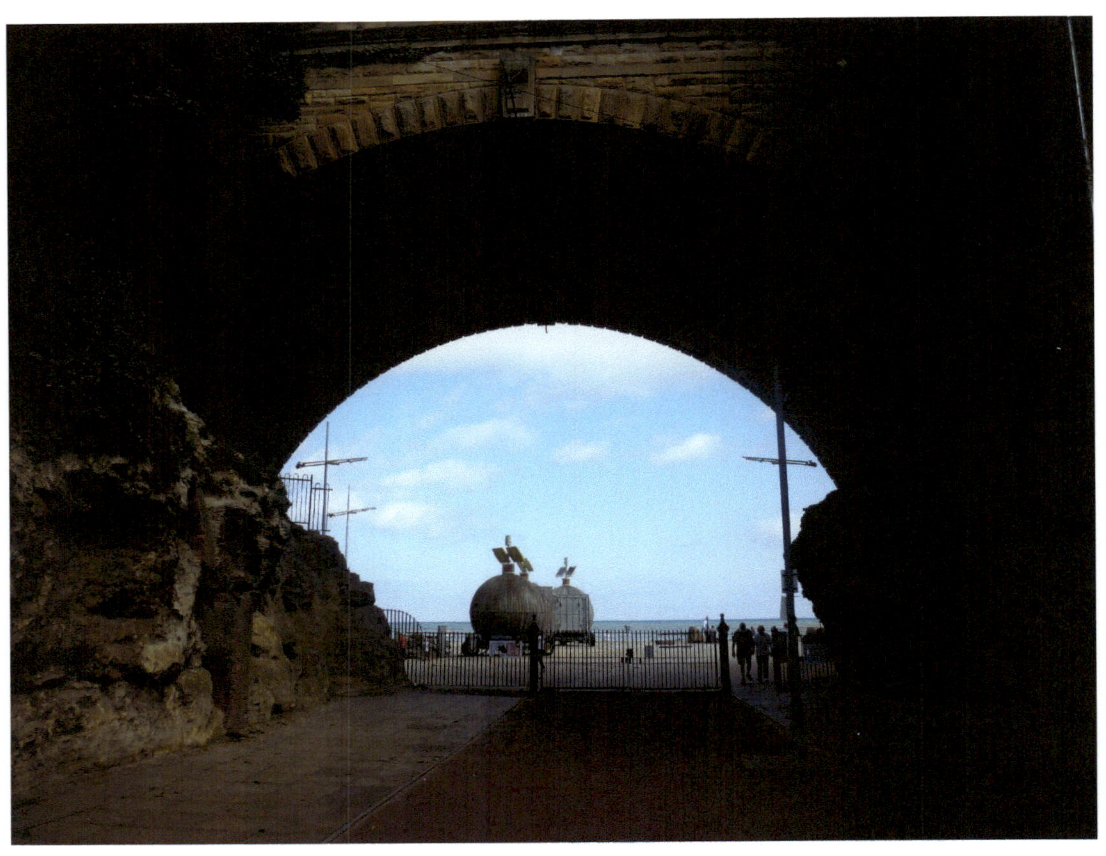

Entrance to the beach.

CHAPTER 24

Washington Old Hall

Washington is a town on the western edges of Sunderland. The original village lies 5 miles from Sunderland's city centre and, as it stands on the River Wear, it has had a connection to the city for over a millennium.

Washington Old Hall is situated in the original village of Washington and a dwelling on the site was first mentioned as far back as 973. Back then the building would have been a wooden structure with a straw roof.

It was William de Hertburn who built the first stone building and constructed the first hall on-site in 1183. After buying the surrounding land William then became William of Wessington, later changing to Washington. His family are the direct ancestors of the first American president, George Washington.

The hall stayed in the Washington family until the fifteenth century when it was sold to a local family called the Mallorys, and then later in 1613 it was bought by William James, the then Bishop of Durham. The bishop pulled down much of the original building and reconstructed the hall to what you see today.

Over the centuries it was used as a home for the wealthy, until the latter part of the eighteenth century when it is recorded that it was converted into tenements for poorer families. During these times the occupants were often housed in cramp, dirty and poor conditions. It is listed in the census of 1891 that thirty-five people occupied this five-bedroom house.

Unfortunately, the building fell into disrepair and in 1936 it was declared as unfit for purpose and stopped housing people. This led to the future of the hall becoming uncertain; demolishing it looked a certainty. Thankfully, the local community stepped in and, with the help of a local teacher called Frederick Hill, they raised the awareness of the hall and worked to restore the building to its former glory. Using the building's American connections to help to raise funds, the hall was restored and reopened in 1956.

In 1977, the American president Jimmy Carter visited Washington Old Hall and famously planted a tree in the grounds, where it still stands proudly today.

With nearly 1,000 years of history there have been many souls come and go, which has led the hall to become a hive of paranormal activity and is well known to local paranormal investigators – myself included.

Reports of an apparition that has been named the 'Grey Lady' have been listed for decades, and she seems to mostly be seen by children. She is often seen and heard weeping, with strong smells of lavender being reported in various areas of the building when she appears.

The sound of a child crying has often been reported with numerous acts of poltergeist activity. These include table and chairs moving. Objects and ornaments have been moved around when there was nobody in the building.

I can give you a first-hand account of what happened when I was lucky enough to spend the night at Washington Old Hall. I was taking part in one of our paranormal investigations as we had been told of the many reports over the years. The small group of six, including myself, were downstairs videoing the area when we heard footsteps from the floor above us. These sounded like heavy footsteps on the wooden boards before they stopped at the far end near the stairs. These were then followed by a loud bang from a door being shut. We quickly got up and ran up the stairs as we knew there was no one in the building. Not only was the room empty, but the doors were all open. None of the doors could have made the slamming that we had all heard.

The night was a busy one as every time we settled down another unexplainable noise was heard in the parts of the hall that were empty. Many years have passed since our visit and I still don't have an explanation for the noises; it still brings me out in goosebumps when I think them.

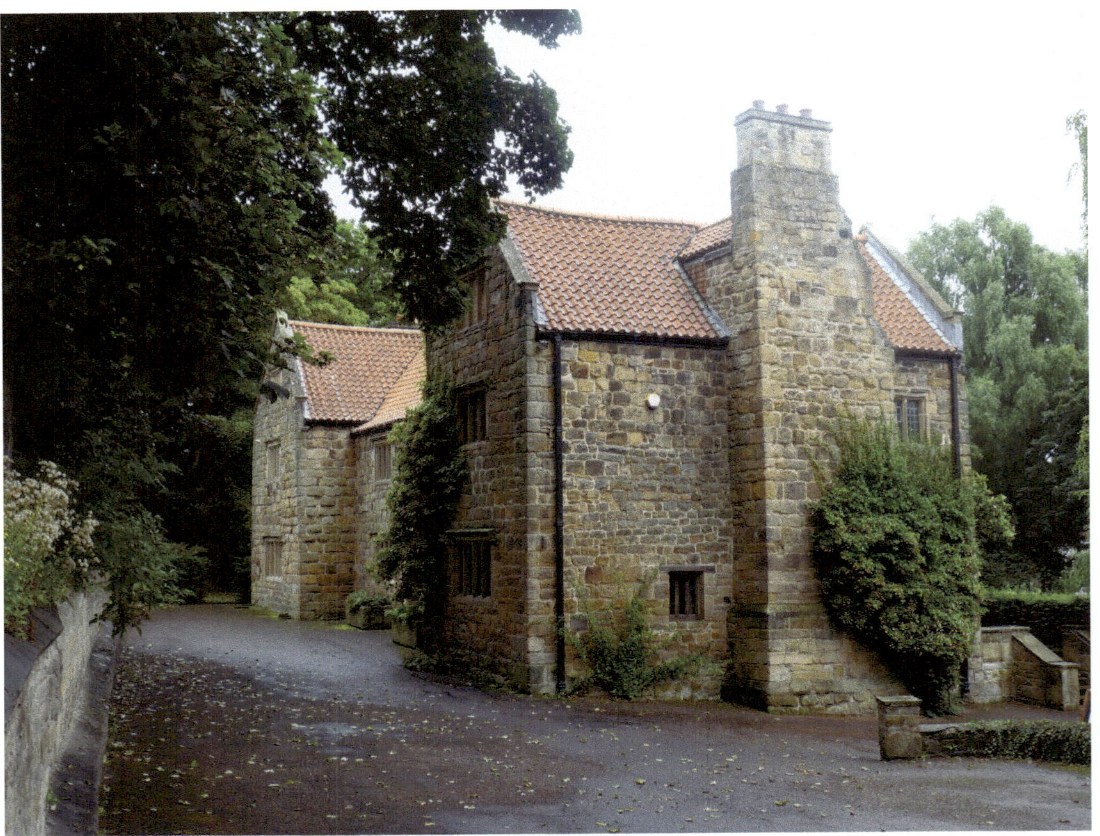

The old hall.

CHAPTER 25

Penshaw Monument

Rising above the banks of the River Wear is Penshaw Hill, with the famous Penshaw Monument sat nobly on top. The monument is a proud symbol of the North East and is easily recognised by North Easterners across the world, along with the Tyne Bridge and the *Angel of the North*.

The hill itself has a history all of its own. It's believed to have been home to an ancient Iron Age fort. In 1644, it would become a camp for Scottish forces that were in the region to attack Newcastle and later fought in the more local Battle of Boldon Hill.

The hill is also mentioned in the northern folk song 'The Lambton Worm' where C. M. Leumane writes that the worm wraps itself around Penshaw Hill ten times. If you are unfamiliar with the story of the Lambton Worm, just ask anyone from the Tyne and Wear area, but please don't be offended when they reply with

Whisht Lads, haad yor gobs,
An Aa'll tell ye's aall an aaful story
Whisht Lads, haad yor gobs,
An' Aa'll tell ye 'boot the warm.

When you stand on top of the hill and look out it is easy to see why the Scots and our Iron Age ancestors used it as a vantage point, as whichever way you look you can see for miles and it is fantastic spot to overlook the whole of Sunderland, all the way to Wearmouth.

The monument's story begins in 1844 when the decision was made to build something to commemorate the life of Lambton, 1st Earl of Durham, who had died four years earlier. It was designed by John and Benjamin Green, who were renowned local architects, a father and son partnership that had previously designed some of the North East's most well-known buildings. Local builder Thomas Pratt was commissioned with bringing the design to life, and the monument opened in 1845. The design was based on the Temple of Hephaestus, a seventh-century Doric temple in Athens. It was constructed using local limestone and still looks impressive today, over 170 years since it was built.

Many of the ghost stories centre around the monument and the apparition of a young boy. He has been spotted wandering around the monument looking lost and wearing old-fashioned clothing – sometimes with a cap and sometimes without. He has also been spotted on top of the monument, which has left people shaken up as they cannot understand how he is up there.

 Paranormal Sunderland

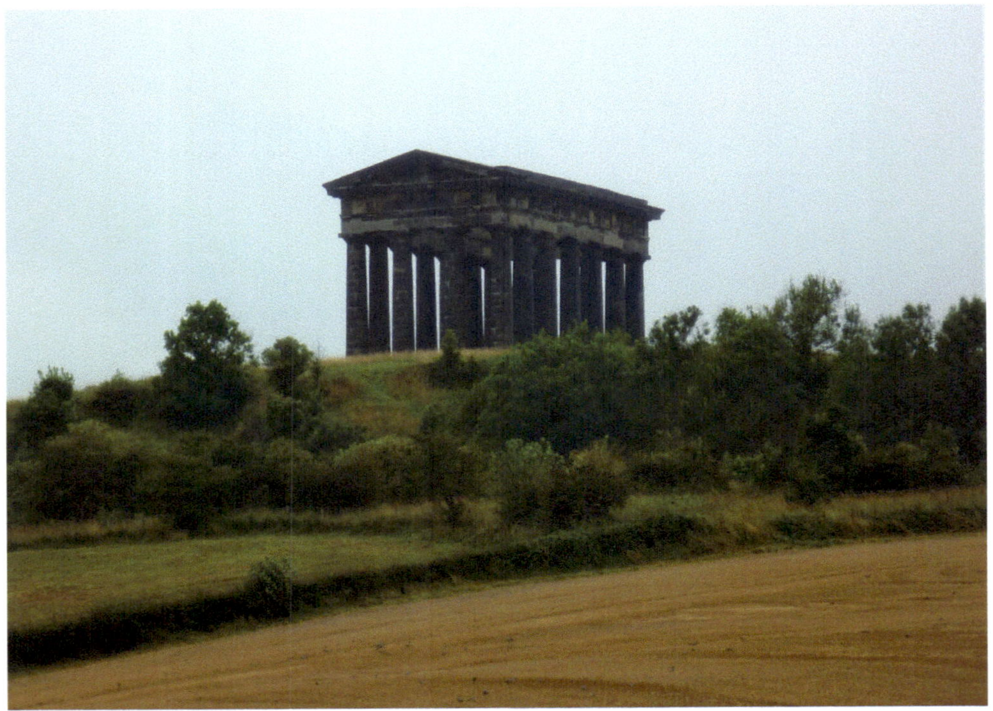

The famous Penshaw Monument.

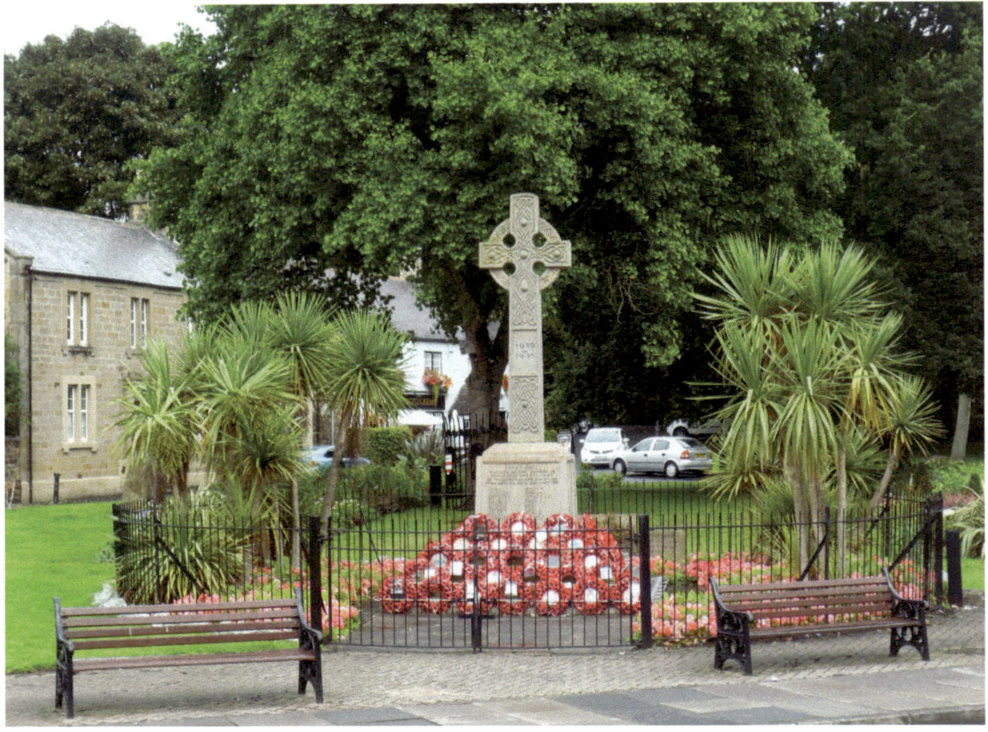

The village green was once home to the pond that was used to dunk witches.

I think the young boy could be linked to a story from 1926 as there are steps up to the top of the monument hidden in one of the columns. These steps used to be open to the public so you could climb to the top and walk around the parapet of the monument to observe the breathtaking scenery. Unfortunately, in this year a teenage boy fell from the top and died from the fall. The steps were immediately closed to the public. It is believed to be this poor soul waving from the top or still wandering around the site.

A white lady has also been seen walking around the hill, but always from a distance. It is said that she walks around and around the hill before disappearing without a trace. There are no stories of who this lady could be, but she appears and disappears near to where we know the Scottish army settled. Whether this is just coincidence, or she had something to do with the Scots, I'll let you decide.

CHAPTER 26

The Wheatsheaf

The Wheatsheaf pub is well known and sits on a busy road junction a few yards from the Wearmouth road bridge. This area has always been a busy traffic throughfare as it was the gateway into Sunderland if you were travelling to or from the north. Dating back centuries, it was the route used by horse and coaches long before the invention of the car, and the area only became busier when the Wearmouth Bridge opened in 1796.

A public house has stood where today's Wheatsheaf is for hundreds of years; however, between the seventeenth and nineteenth centuries it would have been a more traditional coaching inn complete with stables and would play host to the many travellers either visiting or passing through the city.

Today's Wheatsheaf stands on the original ground of its predecessor. It was built in 1898 and is still trading today. However, the Wheatsheaf has a grim history, with one story that seems to have led to a haunting of this building.

During the 1700s, Sunderland had a reputation for its smugglers and highwaymen. The Wheatsheaf had become known for its links to the criminal fraternity, and it would be the ideal place to sell your ill-gotten gains with no questions asked. Behind the scenes was a host of illegal activity including gambling and prostitution. As the story goes, a highwayman had taken a particular liking to one of the young ladies in the bar and mistook her as a lady for hire. After cornering her at the back of the inn, she tried to explain she wasn't for hire and worked behind the bar. The highwayman supposedly took this as an insult, thinking she was making excuses and that his money was not good enough, so he went on to rape her. As she started screaming he silenced her by snapping her neck, killing her instantly. He then hid the body in one of the backrooms and fled.

It wasn't until later that night the horror of the event was discovered when the landlord started looking for his daughter who had disappeared. Her body was discovered and the landlord collapsed, screaming. His daughter was not a young lady, as the highwayman had thought, but still a child just reaching her teenage years.

The landlord offered a reward for information on the highwayman who had cruelly murdered his daughter and swore that he would never rest until he found the person responsible and punished him accordingly. Unfortunately, the landlord went to his grave without ever catching the highwayman – it was rumoured he had fled the country.

All three characters of this story are said to still roam the rooms of the Wheatsheaf. The ghost of young girl has been spotted on numerous occasions sat in the back of the pub crying. The word 'Daddy' has been heard by guests from rooms that are empty and throughout the hotel when staff members are closing down at night.

The figure of a man is sighted mostly in the bar area and upstairs. He is described as an angry spirit that knocks things over and slams doors. Glasses have fallen from the bar and flown off tables for no reason, but this is accompanied by people nearby feeling very intimidated. Could this be the landlord still looking for his daughter?

I have also heard stories from people who are convinced they have seen the highwayman. These reports are that they have seen a dark figure with a hat and cloak and they say he is making a sobbing noise and says 'Sorry' before walking through the walls of the pub, leaving the customers and staff members extremely afraid.

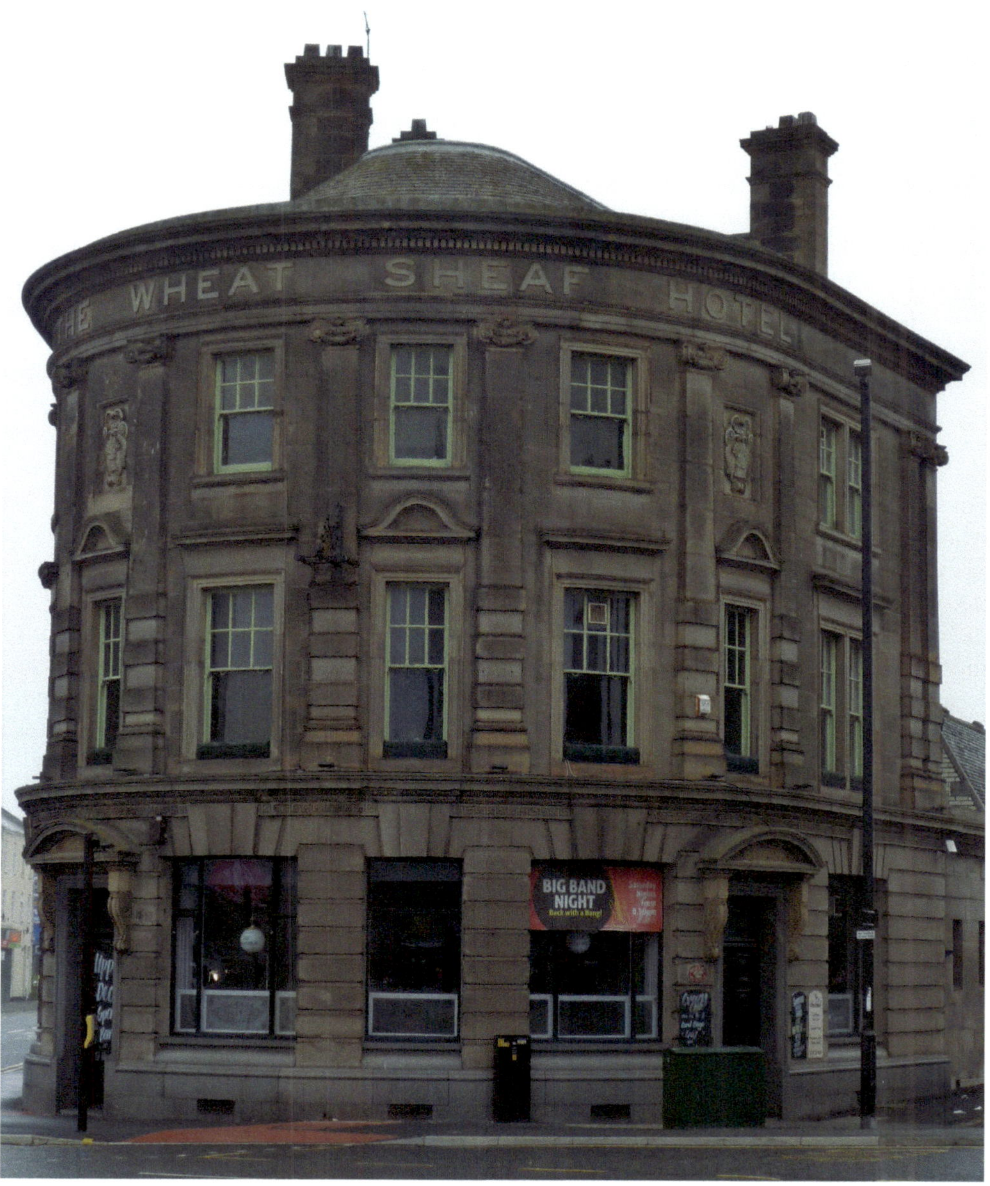

One of Sunderland's oldest coaching inns.

CHAPTER 27

The Witches of Wearside

Over the many years of my research into the paranormal, my obsession had branched out to other subjects. History was already a passion of mine and the multiple stories I have found or been told about witches are quite staggering. These stories come from across the country, all the way from Scotland down to Cornwall and the south coast.

I have been lucky enough to visit and, in some cases, investigate some of the buildings involved with the infamous witch trials, such as Dunbar Townhouse and North Berwick in Scotland, numerous parts of Newcastle, Pendle Hill and Lancaster, and my favourite when I followed in the footsteps of the 'Witchfinder General' Matthew Hopkins through East Anglia and Essex.

Sunderland seems to have mostly missed out on the inhumane witch trials during seventeenth century, when hundreds of innocent people – generally women – were put to death across the UK. Whether this was because Matthew Hopkins didn't come this far north, or the Witch Finder General of Scotland never went further south than Newcastle we will never know. However, Sunderland could be said to have been ahead of its time as two women were trialled for witchcraft in 1446, long before the trials mentioned above.

Mariot de Belton and Isabella Brane were two local ladies that were accused of selling their witchcraft to the young, single ladies of Sunderland by creating potions and spells to bewitch the local men so they could choose a good husband. They were caught and trialled, but this is where the stories differ. Some say they were acquitted, while some stories say that they were found guilty and hanged as witches. If the stories of them being executed are true, this would have taken place on either the Town Moor or Roker Beach. It might explain the ghost story of two ghostly hags that have been seen wandering along Roker Beach late at night and vanish into thin air, only to be replaced by cats that run off into the town.

There is another story of a Wearside witch, this time to the west of the city centre, along the river at Washington, and took place later in the middle of the 1600s. A local lady called Jane Atkinson was accused of being a witch. Her crimes were not listed, although it is said she was accused by her husband to see if her non-stop whining and moaning was the work of the Devil himself.

She was taken to the village pond in Washington and was trialled by 'sink or swim'. Sink or swim was a trial created by witchfinders where your hands and legs were tied up and you were then thrown into water. If you floated you were guilty and, as a witch, you were executed either by fire or hanged by the neck. If you sank and drowned then you were innocent. It was a no-win situation for the poor souls that were accused.

Although Jane Atkinson was 'innocent' and sank to the bottom of the pond and died, her ghost is said to still haunt Washington village green on Halloween, where she is spotted flying around in the night on a broomstick, appearing to be a witch and cursing all those below.

The last story of witches in and around Wearside comes from Seaham. Seaham is a small harbour village 5 miles south down the coastline from the mouth of the Wear. It is well known for Seaham Hall, an eighteenth-century manor house that has a wealth of strange stories about its previous owners, and there are many ghostly tales too as it was used as a hospital after the First World War. Or, for the reason I visit Seaham: Lickety Split, an old-fashioned ice-cream parlour that serves fantastic desserts.

During the time Seaham Hall was an estate and basically covered the whole of the harbour and village area. It is said that a witches' coven of five local women would gather near the cliffs to practise their magic. Their fire would bring unwanted attention from the local gamekeepers and poachers, who were totally unaware that the witches were practising in the area.

One misty night, as the North Sea fog rolled in across the cliffs of Seaham, a group of gamekeepers ventured out to try and catch whoever it was that kept making the fires on the estate. As there had been a spate of poachers seen on the estate, the

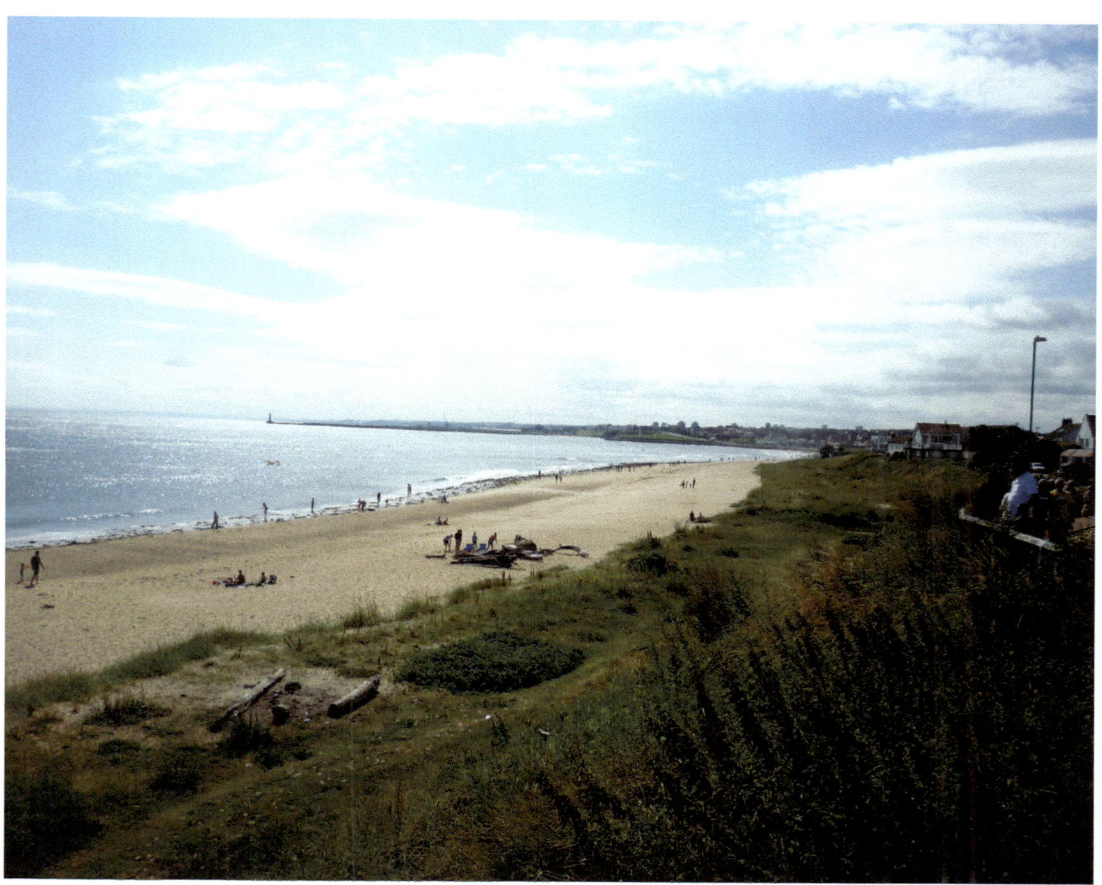

The beach at Sunderland where the apparitions of two witches are seen.

gamekeepers naturally thought the fires belonged to them. As they sneaked up around the group of witches using the fog as cover, they pulled their triggers and shot who they thought were the poachers. It was not until they walked over to the fire that they realised they had actually killed the group of women. Panicking, the gamekeepers quickly dug five graves around the fire and buried the bodies while swearing to each other that they would never speak about the night's events ever again.

The tale goes on to say every member of the group of gamekeepers came to untimely and gruesome deaths. One was caught up in his own animal trap and bled to death, one fell off the nearby cliffs, and it is said that one was so scared of what was happening to his friends that he hanged himself in fear.

Over the years, five trees sprang up over the graves of the witches. Locals say they were never planted and become known as the 'Five Sisters' – an area that you didn't venture by yourself.

As the years went by the story turned into a folklore or an old wives' tale. The problem was that the men employed as gamekeepers or poachers who came from outside the area were unaware of the story, so on foggy nights when the conditions were the same as that fatal night, one of the trees would supposedly turn into a fox. The men would see the fox and give chase, only to be led to the edge of the cliffs where they would fall to their deaths below.

I don't know if the Five Sisters still stand in Seaham or where their exact location is. So, is the story just a good old, spooky story told down the generations? I'll let you decide.

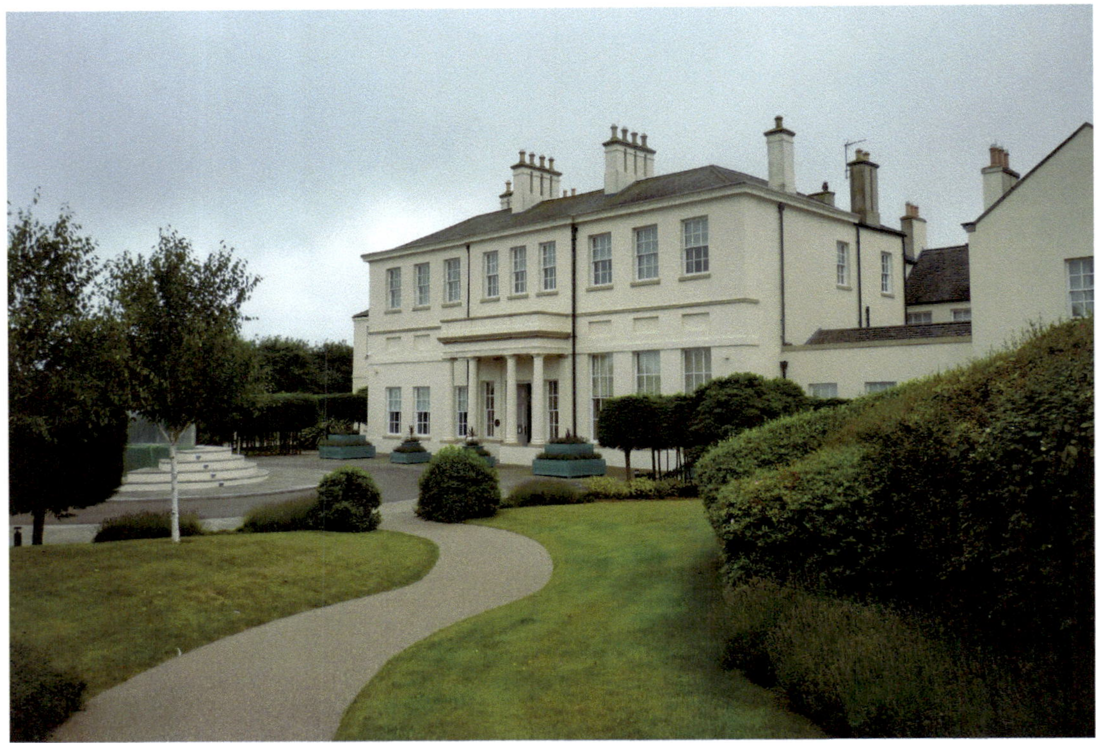

Seaham Hall is the setting for several ghost stories, including the story of the witches.

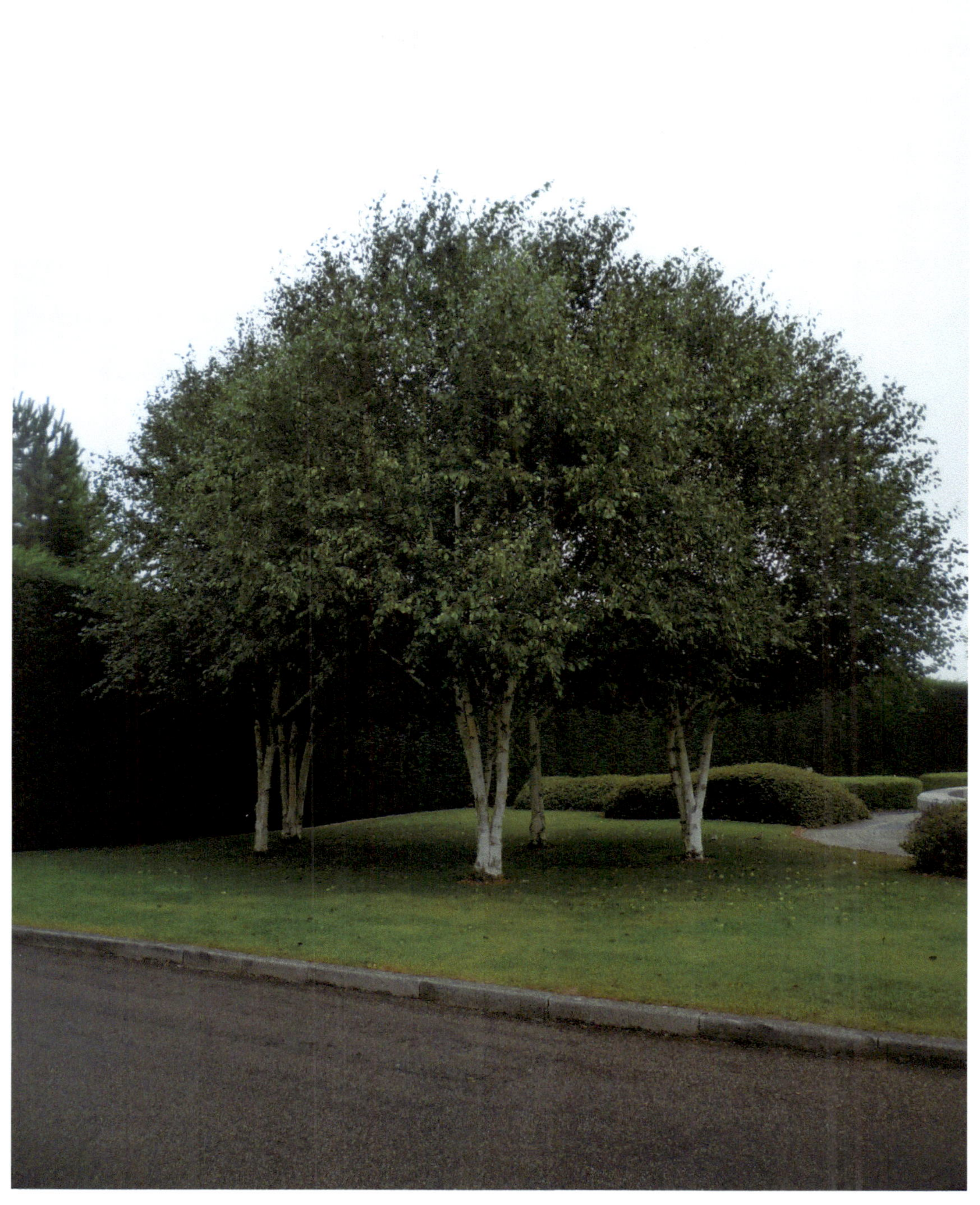

Five trees in the grounds of the hall.

Conclusion

I do hope you have enjoyed this trip through Sunderland's fantastic history and liked reading about its odd tales and strange characters. As I wrote this book I was surprised at how many stories I could have written. I've probably enough to fill another book.

I would like to take this opportunity to thank everyone who has told me their tales over the years and shared their memories with me. Thank you to the kind people who have allowed me into their buildings to take photographs. But most of all, thank you the reader for taking the time to take a look through these pages. I hope some of these stories inspire you to go out and look around this great city to enjoy its heritage. As you walk around look up at the buildings, enjoy their architecture and you never know who or what might be waving at you through the windows.